HV
7936
.R53
R88
2000

WITHDRAWN

$ 15⁰²

THE NEW
POLICE
REPORT
MANUAL

By Devallis Rutledge

MEDIA CENTER
ELIZABETHTOWN COMMUNITY COLLEGE
600 COLLEGE STREET ROAD
ELIZABETHTOWN, KY 42701

D0082209

5858.62

COPPERHOUSE PUBLISHING COMPANY
930 Tahoe Blvd. #602
Incline Village, Nevada 89451
(775) 833-3131 · Fax (775) 833-3133
e-mail info@copperhouse.com
www.copperhouse.com

Your Partner in Education
with
"QUALITY BOOKS AT FAIR PRICES"

The New
POLICE REPORT
MANUAL
2ND Edition

Copyright © 2000, 1996, 1993, 1989, 1986 by Copperhouse Publishing Company

All rights reserved. No portion of this book may be reprinted or reproduced in any manner without prior written permission of the publisher; except for brief passages which may be quoted in connection with a book review and only when source credit is given.

Library of Congress Catalog Number 84-70351
ISBN 0-928916-13-9 Paper Text Edition

2 3 4 5 6 7 8 9 10

Printed in the United States of America.

THE *NEW* POLICE REPORT MANUAL

Here's what some of the people who know police
work are saying about:

THE *NEW* POLICE REPORT MANUAL . . .

*"What a relief—no dull grammar or spelling
lessons; no cumbersome rules to memorize! Officers
actually enjoy reading* **THE *NEW* POLICE
REPORT MANUAL.** *And the results are amaz-
ing—greatly improved reports with* **less** *effort! A
'must' for every Police Academy in the U.S."*

> Norman Cleaver, Ass't Dean, Director
> Basic Police Academy
> Criminal Justice Training Center
> Golden West College
> Huntington Beach, California

*"Finally, an easy-to-read book that makes police
report writing so simple and effective it's almost a
pleasure to write reports!"*

> Art Courteau
> Training Officer
> Costa Mesa, CA Police Department

"THE NEW POLICE REPORT MANUAL has simplified an overcomplicated task for the law enforcement officer. Unlike the stiff grammar books which previously passed for report writing manuals, this new work provides a fluid approach to effective narrative writing, without boring the reader with unwelcome talk about parts of speech, punctuation and spelling.

"THE NEW POLICE REPORT MANUAL makes an outstanding contribution to law enforcement. I predict that it will cause positive changes in police procedure. Here's hoping it finds its way into many law enforcement agencies, police academies and classrooms, and many individuals' hands!"

Bruce A. Hand
Administration of Criminal
Justice Consultant

"All peace officers—including supervisors—should be required to read this book! It's a one-of-a-kind report writing manual, far superior to anything else that's been written in this area. Officers who follow the suggestions for reducing work while improving their reports will not only save themselves a lot of headaches, they will also make the work of criminal defense attorneys very, very difficult."

Walt Posey
Attorney at Law
Police Science Instructor
Formerly, Detective Sergeant
Anaheim Police Department

"Long overdue! A cop-turned-prosecutor tells other cops, in plain language that's easy to read and understand, how to write reports that everyone can easily read and understand. I strongly recommend this unique manual to all peace officers and security personnel!"

Maury Evans
Deputy District Attorney
Formerly, FBI Special Agent
Formerly, Chief of Security
JC Penneys

"When I was asked to review THE NEW POLICE REPORT MANUAL, I said to myself, 'Not another manual on such a dry topic—I don't need another English lesson!' But what a surprise when I started reading it! I enjoyed it!—in fact, I didn't put it down until I had read every word. I would never have believed anyone could write a stimulating book on report writing, and without a single English lesson, but here it is.

"This book convincingly points out the problems, from the prosecutor's viewpoint, of many reporting practices we've all been guilty of using everyday. I wholeheartedly recommend it to everyone who has to write investigative reports. The examples are great—the whole book is simply excellent!"

Marv Engquist
Robbery-Homicide Investigator
Los Angeles Police Department

TO TELL THE TRUTH . . .

Not all of my reviews were 100% favorable. Like everybody else who has written what he thinks is a good book, I hoped reviewers would agree with me. And like everybody else who wants his book to succeed, I sent the manuscript to people whose opinions should carry great weight with members of my intended audience; I asked them for their honest appraisals. I'm grateful for their approving comments.

Unlike other authors, I didn't get all completely-favorable reviews. One of the people I asked to review the manuscript—a training sergeant at a peace officers' academy—said this:

I was not impresssed with the first chapter of your book and would not have read further if I had not agreed to give you an opinion of the entire book. But after reading the second chapter, I was really interested. As the examples progressed, I began to realize that I have done everything you point out as being wrong, and I had always thought of myself as a good report writer! The remainder of the book was equally impressive. Then I went back to find out why Chapter 1 had turned me off.

At first, I had found myself agitated when you kept saying, "your bad report." It was just too personal and too critical. I would have felt more comfortable if you had kept it impersonal and let me see gradually that I really am the one you are talking about—I form that conclusion quickly enough after reading a few examples! And I found myself wanting to read more, and began playing a mental game of trying to guess the correct answer. Most of the time, your correct example was even easier than mine.

I'm glad this sergeant was completely candid in his response, because if my intended audience won't read the book, cover to cover, then I've failed to meet my first objective in writing it.

So I gave the sergeant's suggestion considerable thought. But I decided that rather than changing Chapter 1 to an impersonal statement, I would let you know, up front, what his overall reaction was, and then go ahead and print what I had written.

I don't want to hurt your feelings . . . I want to help you get better at doing your job, so I can get better at doing mine. Just as **you** need the help of responsible citizens to succeed at your task of identifying and arresting offenders, I need the help of responsible officers to succeed in my job of convicting the criminals you arrest.

A part of being responsible is recognizing that you can't do **anything** better (including writing police reports) until you first find out what's wrong with the way you're doing it now. And neither you nor anyone else is going to be motivated to change an established reporting habit unless something convinces you that there are logical, compelling reasons to change, and that these reasons apply to you, personally, and not just to everyone else.

That's what the first chapter is all about. And that's why I've written this book in an informal, person-to-person style. I'm talking to **you**—not to some typical composite officer. A little initial criticism shouldn't turn you off, as long as you realize it's put there to turn you **on** to the need for improvement. I hope you'll look at it that way—that's the only way it's meant.

Devallis Rutledge

CONTENTS

WHAT'S THE PROBLEM?

I had been a cop about a week or so when I wrote my first report. I'd been riding with a senior patrol officer, waiting for the next academy class to begin, and picking up a little OJT. We had recovered a stolen bicycle—nothing too complicated—and he told me to try my hand at the report.

I pecked at the typewriter a few minutes and handed him my report. He read it and just stood there shaking his head. He could see he was going to have to show me how to write a **real** report.

He showed me. I read his version—which was about twice as long as mine—and just stood there shaking my head. I asked the same question you probably asked the first time someone "corrected" your reports: "Why do we write like **that?**"

You probably got the same answer I did: "Because that's the way we've always done it."

The problem is, the way we've always done it is wrong. I didn't know that as a rookie cop. I thought maybe the prosecutors or the courts needed it done that way for some reason, so I was content to learn how to write a **real** police report, and I wrote that way as long as I was a cop.

A few years later, when I became a prosecutor and saw that cops were still writing the same way, I began to look for the mysterious reason I had always supposed existed somewhere in the courthouse. I looked high and low. I looked while reading reports to determine whether or not I could issue complaints; I looked as I used reports in pre-trial motions, in plea bargaining sessions, and in trials. From my point of view as a prosecutor, I couldn't find the reason anywhere.

So I asked around. I checked with other prosecutors, judges, probation officers, police science instructors, academy instructors—even a couple of chiefs. I can now assure you, without any reservations, that the only excuse for the way police reports are written is because that's the way we've always done it, and no one has bothered to ask why.

And it isn't just a local problem here in my county or there in yours. I've probably seen over 5000 reports, from about fifty different departments, and a dozen different states. They're all about the same. They follow a fairly standard formula for writing a real police report, the way we've always done it.

And as I said before, the way we've always done it is wrong. Now, I don't say that just to be complaining. In fact, I recognize, along with everyone else, that there's less to complain about in today's police officer than ever before. In spite of what your captain can tell you about the good old days, cops have never been more proficient than they are now. You've got more education and better training, and you're working under more stringent requirements from the department, the courts, and the community, than any cop who had that badge before you.

The problem is, while you've been getting better and better at doing most of your police work, you've just been getting worse at writing about it. For the most part, you're not personally to blame. You've been trained to write by the police formula, and you've taken it on faith that there must be a good reason to do it that way. And now you're so used to it that it comes automatically, just like a second language.

The problem is, reports shouldn't be written (nor dictated) in a second language—they should be done in the one language we all have in common: plain old everyday English. I know you probably think that's what you've been using, but I suspect that before we're through, you may change your mind. And I hope, for your sake and for mine, that you may also change your writing habits.

I've said twice now that the way we've always written police reports is wrong. What's the matter with it? Just about everything. While some reports are too brief, most are too long. They're difficult to read and understand. They're ambiguous and conclusionary. They omit important facts and overemphasize trivial ones. The vocabulary is stilted and absurdly misused; the style is awkward, unnatural and unconvincing. The result is that most police reports don't do their job.

What job are they supposed to do? **Communicate.** When you sit down to write a crime or arrest report, you do it for one basic purpose—to communicate your information about the incident to the people who read your report—not to **impress** them, not to **amuse,** not to **entertain,** and not to **confuse**— just to **communicate.**

You don't write a police report to show off your education and your giant vocabulary or to showcase your literary style. You don't do it to prove that you've learned the official rules of grammar so well that you can cleverly avoid dangling prepositions and split infinitives. Your only legitimate purpose in writing a report is to communicate information. If your report communicates clearly, accurately, completely and convincingly to everyone who reads it, you've written well; if it doesn't, then you've wasted your time writing it, and the readers have wasted their time trying to read it.

And consider this: when you fail to communicate effectively to those of us in law enforcement who depend on your reports, you're doing the criminal a favor. The less useful your reports are to other officers, to prosecutors, to prosecution witnesses, and to jurors and judges, the more beneficial they are to criminal defendants and their attorneys.

If follow-up investigators can't read your reports, they may have to duplicate some of the work you've already done, just to find out information you already knew but didn't communicate. Witnesses who can't depend on your reports to refresh their recollection when testifying may give incomplete or inaccurate testimony. Judges and jurors who have trouble reading and understanding what you've written may decide that you were trying to **conceal** something, and they may then distrust your testimony.

And look at some of the problems a bad report causes me, the prosecutor. If your report is bad enough, I may have to decline to file a complaint (if you've arrested someone and put him in jail, where does that leave you and your department?). Even if I can decipher enough of a poorly-written report to issue a complaint, I may still have problems figuring out whom to subpena for trial if you haven't clearly communicated **who** can testify to **what**.

Or take an even more common problem. Have you ever been to a "plea bargaining" session after the complaint is filed and watched the prosecutor "negotiate" cases with defense lawyers? Do you know what the defense lawyer uses against me **more often than any other thing** in his client's behalf? Your report!

Doesn't that seem ironic? After you literally bust your tail catching some criminal and locking him up, you sit down at the desk and compose something he uses to get out. Certainly, you don't **intend** for your report to be more useful to the defense than it is to the prosecutor. The problem is, that's how it turns out, in an unbelievable number of cases.

When I sit down and talk to defense lawyers, I don't often hear about any legitimate defenses your arrestee has. And unless I'm dealing with a brand new public defender, I don't have to listen to what a nice guy this defendant really is, and how I ought to reduce or dismiss because this will look bad on his application for a security clearance. What I hear more often than any other argument is this:

> *"Have you looked at the police report? Do you believe this piece of junk? I can't wait to get the officer on the stand in front of a jury with this report! Do you really want to take this case to trial?"*

If I haven't already done it, I read the report. Then I see why the defense attorney is so happy with your writing. It doesn't make sense. You've contradicted the complaining witness. You've left out critical facts. You've stuffed in too many conclusions and ambiguities. You've misused unfamiliar words so that the sentence comes out embarrassingly comical. You've written in such a phony style that everything you say sounds unrealistic. You've written a piece of junk. You've created half a dozen defenses for the criminal you arrested. **Whose side are you on?**

Now I have to consider the effect your report is going to have at trial: it's going to confuse the jurors; it may impeach my witnesses—including you; it's going to hold you up to ridicule; it's going to increase the chances of an acquittal. So now I do something I don't like to do: I reduce the charge or the sentence in exchange for a guilty plea. Not because your arrest wasn't good, but because your report was bad. Many reports are so bad that the prosecution would be better off if you hadn't written **anything**.

Let's face it. It's not enough for you to be good at **apprehending** criminals—you've also got to be good at helping me with my job of **convicting** them, by giving me a report I can use against the guy you've busted, instead of the other way around.

You can't take much satisfaction in arresting criminals if you can't get a complaint filed, or make the right charges stick, just because you're no good at writing a report. Like it or not, as long as you're a cop, you're going to be a writer. And no matter how good

This is police work.

And so is this . . .

. . . and this.

you are in the field, you're not going anywhere if too
many of your arrests wind up getting thrown out by
the D.A. or the jury.

Got the picture by now? Writing reports is a crucial
part of your job. And the problem is, the way we've
always done it has created a lot of unnecessary problems—for you, for me, and for the community we
work for. So I'm going to ask you, in the remaining
pages of this book, to put a little less effort into your
reports.

No, that wasn't a typographical error. I **meant** to
say a little **less** effort. One reason your reports are so
hard to read and understand is because you put too
much effort into writing—you're making more work
out of it than it needs. You're trying so hard to follow
the formula for writing a "real" police report, and
you're making such an effort to show everybody that
you've learned a bunch of impressive-sounding
words, that you've gone way past the work level you
needed to communicate your knowledge.

My suggestions in the next few chapters are aimed
at making it easier for you to write a report and easier
for me to read and use it. Since I agree with the adage
"Work smarter, not harder," I'm not going to ask
more of you—I'm going to ask **less**.

(To those of you who may have tried to read a book
on report writing before, please don't leave me yet. If
you looked through the table of contents, you may
have noticed that this isn't just another remedial

English textbook disguised as a report writing manual. I promise you, there isn't a single grammar lesson from cover to cover—not one mention of subject-predicate agreement or faulty parallelism. In fact, there are some suggestions later on that you might even call "antigrammar" lessons.

(And if you've counted the pages, you'll see that I've kept this book to a readable length by not trying to throw into it everything I could think of that might be used for filling. I'm not going to try to follow the formula for writing a "real" textbook, simply because that's the way we've always done it. I'm just going to try to communicate with you about how to make your reports easier to write, easier to read, and easier for **our** side to use. Fair enough?)

All of the examples I've used throughout the book are edited from actual reports that have crossed my desk. I've changed some names and addresses.

□

THE BEST APPROACH

Remember in the old cops-and-robbers movies how the police made a carstop? They pulled the police car around **in front** of the car they were stopping, and then walked **back** toward the driver. Of course, it didn't take too many shootings for the real police to figure out the disadvantages of that kind of approach. Since then, everybody knows that you stop **behind** your suspect, leave yourself an offset safety corridor on your approach side, and walk toward the driver from the rear, so you can see him better than he can see you. And then you stand slightly to his rear at the car window, so he would have to turn and twist before he could aim a gun at you.

Of course the old approach was better if your objective was to prevent the car from driving away once you stopped. The present approach assumes that you put your personal safety above the importance of keeping a stopped car from taking off again. So if your first objective is to stay alive, stopping to the rear is the best approach.

The best approach to report writing depends on your objective, too. If you think using police jargon and impressing the reader are more important than communicating clearly, you'll want to stay with the old approach. If you agree with me that the objective of writing a report is to communicate information, I have some suggestions, as a reader, on the best approach for accomplishing that objective. And remember, it's the **reader** you've got to communicate **to.**

Before we get to some specific problems, let's spend a few minutes thinking about your general approach to writing. I classify the writing styles I've seen into two basic approaches: **natural** and **artificial.** The approach I call "natural" is the writing style that's closest to the way people talk to each other in the course of everyday communications—it's basic, simple and straightforward. The other writing style bears little resemblance to the way most people really communicate—it's overcomplicated, obscure, indirect, stilted, and unfamiliar. Some people like to call this "formal" writing, but since I believe in being straightforward, I just call it "artificial."

Have you noticed that most people have a **speaking** language and a different **writing** language? Did you ever wonder why? In fact, many of us have **two** speaking languages—the one we use all the time, everyday, and the one we only use with certain audiences, like strangers, supervisors, and our social "betters." This latter speaking language is usually a lot like the phony writing language—it's made up of the Sunday-go-to-meetin' vocabulary we only dust off for special occasions and wouldn't dream of using for everyday speech.

Why do you suppose we have these two different levels of speaking? Probably to serve two different purposes. Our plain old everyday straight talk we use when all we're trying to do is communicate; the "formal" line isn't really as much for communicating as for impressing people—letting them know we're not uneducated simpletons. Why else would someone say something like "He personifies the quintessence of parsimonious existence," when all they mean is "He's stingy"? One of those sentences is designed to **impress**, one to **communicate**.

So. The approach you're going to use to stop a car, or to say something, or to write something, depends on what you're trying to do. Since the objective of a police report is to communicate information as clearly and as accurately as possible, you should be using the approach that's best calculated to do that: the

There's a wrong way . . .

. . . and there's a right way.

It all depends on what your objective is.

natural approach—using the basic language that we do most of our communicating in.

I know you can't write reports exactly the same way you talk—there are legitimate reasons for leaving out profanity, radio code talk, street slang, and other words and phrases that would generally be either offensive or unfamiliar to your readers. But a good objective for your writing is to try to come close to the ease and simplicity of everyday speech. When you sit down to write the details of an arrest, imagine yourself about to tell the story to a civilian friend. Then, when you start to write something, just ask yourself: "If I were talking, instead of writing, is that how I'd say it?" If your answer is **no**, you were just about to write artificially again. If your answer is **yes**, go ahead and write it—now you're communicating!

It's possible you may get some resistance to a change from artificial to natural writing. You have to remember that some of your superior officers and some prosecutors have grown accustomed to what they have been told was the "objective, professional style" of report writing. Some of them have endorsed—even taught—the artificial approach, and the oldest habits are the hardest to break.

However, the oldest habits are often the ones that need breaking the most, and the superstition that police reports ought to be written in as impersonal and stilted a fashion as possible is overdue for the historical museum. Every supervisor worth his salt knows that a part of supervising is looking closely at existing procedures and asking: "Why do we **do** this? Why do we do it **this way?**" If he doesn't know the reason, and if he can't find anyone who does, maybe it's because there **is** no reason—some things just get started, and copied, and perpetuated, and no one ever bothers asking why.

I can assure you, at least from the point of view of approving complaints and getting convictions (can you think of a more important point of view for police reports?), that there is **no** justifiable reason for preferring an awkward, stilted, artificial method of writing to a straightforward, natural one. If someone tries to give you some "good" reasons for avoiding basic everyday language in your reports, see how the reasons fit in with the fact that your purpose in writing is to communicate information to the reader. (Clue: They won't fit.)

Some English teachers and advocates of "formal" writing may tell you I'm full of baloney. They're entitled to their opinions. But English teachers don't have to issue criminal complaints on the basis of your reports. They don't have to do battle with a defense attorney who can raise half a dozen motions to suppress and dismiss from a poorly-written report. They don't have to try the case to a jury of naive citizens who think that every ambiguity in an officer's report is a basis for reasonable doubt. They don't have to **use** your reports to get their job done. I do.

There are books on report writing alongside this one in the bookstore (mostly written by people who don't have to use your reports) that talk about "formal" writing as a "reflection on your education, expertise and professionalism." They're entitled to their opinions. But if I needed to know something about your education (I don't), I'd ask for your transcript. I don't want you writing a report to show off your education. I want to know things about elements of the crime, probable cause for an arrest, and evidence of guilt. Can you picture me arguing to a jury that they should disregard the fact that they can't understand your report and convict the defendant because "the officer's formal writing technique clearly reflects an admirable education"?

And as for expertise and professionalism, those don't come through in a report that nobody can read and understand. They show up in a report that's clear, correct, and convincing. I don't really think anyone wants to argue that the more artificial your writing becomes, the more professional you will appear. And remember, your objective isn't to promote an appearance—it's just to communicate.

Like a fast-talking used-car salesman, that word "professional" snags a lot of people and sells them on something they'd never buy if they just thought twice. But people in all occupations like to think their work is so specialized that only a professional can do it. As part of giving their occupation a mystique and setting it aside as belonging to a certain kind of specialist, they create a technical jargon that only others of their group can use and understand. Once a worker has mastered the jargon, he's a "professional." Now you can tell him from an amateur by the way he talks (mainly, you can't understand him anymore).

It's only natural that those who bought the most stock in this line of "professionalism" might be the last to admit it wasn't really a sound investment. But don't worry. You don't need artificial reporting in an unfamiliar language to make you a professional. If you can do your job of enforcing laws, preventing crime, apprehending offenders, and writing informative reports about your activities in basic English, you're a professional, and no amount of "formal writing skill" is going to improve on that.

Cops are by no means alone in substituting a confusing writing style for a clear one, and they don't come close to being the worst perpetrators. I think everyone would agree that people in my profession—lawyers—are the world's worst communicators, followed closely by government bureaucrats, corporate executives, insurance underwriters, and bankers. And just about everyone is guilty to some degree. Even the simplest business letters and advertising circulars have become unnesessarily complicated.

Here, so you can have a laugh at the rest of us and
not feel too alone, are some samples of the ridiculous
writing being done in other occupations. After you've
seen the difference a natural approach makes in these
illustrations, maybe a few changes in police report
writing won't seem too hard to accept.

This was obviously written by a lawyer:

> *In the event that the requisite number of
> shares of a corporation are voted to approve
> its merger or consolidation with another
> corporation, domestic or foreign, any
> holder of voting or nonvoting shares who
> did not vote any or all of the shares which
> he was entitled to vote in favor of the
> merger or consolidation at the meeting at
> which it was approved may require the cor-
> poration of which he is a shareholder to pur-
> chase the shares which he did not vote in
> favor of the merger or consolidation and to
> pay him their fair market value.*

If you read it slowly enough, two or three times,
you can figure it out. But wouldn't it be easier for
everyone if the lawyer had just written:

> *If a shareholder votes against a merger and
> the merger goes through, he can make the
> corporation buy his stock at market price.*

And while we're on the subject of corporations,
look at these two quotations from the California Corporations Code. After you read the first one, see if

you think the writer had a lapse in memory before he
wrote the second one, three pages later in the Code:

> *There is substantial immediate need to
> educate the people of the State of California
> to understand how the law is responsive to
> their needs, works to the general good and
> protects the rights of all.*

So far, so good, right? But then:

> *Every nonprofit corporation, during any
> period or periods such corporation is
> deemed to be a "private foundation" as
> defined in Section 509 of the Internal
> Revenue Code of 1954 as amended by Sec-
> tion 101 of The Tax Reform Act of 1969 (all
> references in this section to the Internal
> Revenue Code shall refer to such code as
> amended by such act), shall distribute its
> income for each taxable year (and principal,
> if necessary) at such time and in such man-
> ner as not to subject such corporation to tax
> under Section 4942 of such code (as
> modified by paragraph (3) of subsection (1)
> of Section 101 of the Tax Reform Act of
> 1969), and such corporation shall not
> engage in any act of self-dealing as defined
> in subsection (d) of Section 4941 of such
> code (as modified by paragraph (2) of
> subsection (1) of Section 101 of the Tax
> Reform Act of 1969), retain any excess*

> *business holdings as defined in subsection*
> *(c) of Section 4943 of such code, make any*
> *investments in such manner as to subject*
> *such corporation to tax under Section 4944*
> *of such code, or make any taxable expen-*
> *diture as defined in subsection (d) of Sec-*
> *tion 4945 of such code (as modified by*
> *paragraph (5) of subsection (1) of Section*
> *101 of the Tax Reform Act of 1969).*

If you were watching the punctuation marks, you noticed that all of that incomprehensible effort "to educate the people" was crammed into **one** sentence—a 223-word sentence! And all it would have taken in straight talk was this:

> *Nonprofit corporations that qualify as*
> *"private foundations" under the Internal*
> *Revenue Code have to handle their business*
> *affairs in such a way that they don't have to*
> *pay any taxes under the following code sec-*
> *tions: 4941(d); 4942; 4943(c); 4944 and*
> *4945(d). All of these sections have been*
> *amended by the 1969 Tax Reform Act, Sec-*
> *tion 101.*

There you have two sentences totalling 56 words—25% of the original length. What's more important, the shorter version can be **read**; the actual code section has to be **deciphered**. Not a very good way, is it, to help the people understand how good and responsive the law is?

While I was working on the first few pages of this book, I got a "personal invitation" in the mail to accept a department store credit card. Printed in big, black letters at the bottom of the "retail charge agreement" was this notice:

> *Any holder of this consumer credit contract is subject to all claims and defenses which the debtor could assert against the seller of goods or services obtained pursuant hereto or with the proceeds hereof. Recovery hereunder by the debtor shall not exceed amounts paid by the debtor hereunder.*

What does that mean? It means the people at the store could sell their interest in the contract, and the new owner would stand in the store's shoes. If you make a claim against them, you can't get back more than you've paid.

Why didn't the department store just say what they meant in a way that would easily communicate their message to the maximum number of readers? I don't know. I suspect that whoever wrote their notice was preoccupied with impressing someone and didn't care too much whether he communicated with his readers.

I could throw in excerpts from my auto insurance policy and my home mortgage and last year's "simplified" income tax instructions and hundreds of other things, but I hope you've gotten the message. Police officers aren't the only ones who could put less effort into writing and get better results. Incidentally, you may have noticed that federal bureaucrats are now under orders to write regulations in plain, understandable English, and a few banks and insurance companies are making advertising mileage out of the claim that their contracts and policies are now written in basic, simple language "that people can actually read and undertand!" So my asking you to take that approach in **your** writing isn't as revolutionary as you might have thought. Let's move on to your reports and try it out.

□

"I" WON'T BITE

The first thing you need to do to shake artificial writing and become more natural is to decide who you really are. Everybody had at least one English teacher along the way who issued a commandment that you aren't allowed to refer to yourself in writing as "I" or "me." They never told you **why** you couldn't do it—just that it wasn't permitted. Maybe it isn't permitted in English 1A, but remember, you're not writing for your English teachers anymore. You're writing for people who have to depend on your reports to make the criminal justice system work.

And don't get fooled by people who tell you your

reports won't be "objective" if you break down and use little words like "I" and "me." In the first place, you're not fooling anybody when you refer to yourself as "this officer," or "reporting detective," or "assigned officer," or any of those other aliases you've been writing under. Sure, you'll slow your reader down somewhat as he mentally notes each time he reads "reporting officer" it means the same thing as if you'd simply said "I." But how does that kind of reading obstruction improve objectivity?

In the second place, objectivity isn't the all-important writing goal that some people unquestioningly assume it is. There are times when your state of mind is also important (for example, when you're explaining why you drew your weapon, or why you stopped a car or searched someone)—that's **subjectivity.** As long as you're paying proper attention to accuracy and thoroughness, you don't need to worry about objectivity—it will be taken care of. You unnecessarily sacrifice readability and believability in the name of "objectivity" when you disguise yourself as "this officer" and try to fool the readers into thinking **you** weren't really there—that the arrest was really made by some mysterious, detached observer named "this officer," who was just using your eyes and ears at the time!

The fact is, when those of us who use your report need to be convinced of what you've written, or need to convince a defense attorney or a judge or a juror that you know what you're talking about, we don't want something that sounds like a third-hand report—we want a good, solid, eyewitness account by someone who can forthrightly say: "I saw him throw the knife," or "I heard a woman screaming." You don't strengthen your objectivity by writing under an assumed name; you just weaken the convincing force of everything you say.

Now that you have that "objectivity" myth in proper perspective, compare the artificial with the natural in these examples. Ask yourself which one is easier to **write,** and which is easier to **read.** And remember that your test question before you **write** something is "How would I say it?"

EXAMPLES

ARTIFICIAL: *He said he would talk to Reporting Officer.*

NATURAL: *He said he would talk to me.*

□   □   □

ARTIFICIAL: *This officer searched the room.*

NATURAL: *I searched the room.*

□   □   □

ARTIFICIAL: *The flashlight was the one belonging to this officer.*

NATURAL: *The flashlight was mine.*

□   □   □

ARTIFICIAL: *Officer Bacon and the Undersigned Officer effected a rendezvous at First and Maple.*

NATURAL: *I met Officer Bacon at First and Maple.*

☐   ☐   ☐

ARTIFICIAL: *Assigned Officer returned to Assigned's unit and retrieved Assigned's citation book.*

NATURAL: *I got my citation book from the police car.*

☐   ☐   ☐

ARTIFICIAL: *Assigned Officer radioed his location and drew his baton.*

NATURAL: *I radioed my location and drew my baton.*

☐   ☐   ☐

And look at the further difficulties you can get into when you start calling yourself "he":

EXAMPLE

ARTIFICIAL: *Assigned Officer, referring to his "Miranda" card, read him his rights, whereupon he became visibly nervous, and his hands began to shake.*

Whose card was it? Whose rights? Who got nervous?

Whose hands shook? Try this:

NATURAL: *When I read his rights from my "Miranda" card, I saw his hands shaking.*

Here's another kind of communication gap you create unnecessarily with this funny writing:

EXAMPLE

ARTIFICIAL: *Assigned Officers Bennett, Carter and myself arrived first. Assigned Officer saw that the light was red.*

Which one of the three "Assigned Officers" saw the light?

NATURAL: *Officers Bennett and Carter and I arrived first. I saw that the light was red.*

☐   ☐   ☐

And if single-sentence comparisons don't illustrate the problem adequately for you, look at the difference when sentences become paragraphs:

EXAMPLE

ARTIFICIAL: *The assigned officer was dispatched to Community Hospital. Assigned Officer made contact with nurses who directed the assigned officer to the victim. The*

> *assigned officer identified the
> victim as John Falner. The
> assigned officer asked Mr.
> Falner the circumstances of
> the stabbing. The victim
> related to the assigned officer
> that there were four suspects.
> The assigned officer spoke
> with Dr. Eaker, who advised
> the assigned officer that he
> would give the assigned of-
> ficer a full report shortly.*

You see how ridiculous that becomes? And when a series of such paragraphs form a report, the problem is magnified still more. There are some other problems with this paragraph besides the useless repetition of "assigned officer," but those are the subjects of later suggestions. For now, look at the difference just substituting in "I" and "me" can make:

NATURAL: *I was dispatched to Community Hospital. I made
contact with nurses who
directed me to the victim. I
identified the victim as John
Falner. I asked Mr. Falner
the circumstances of the stab-
bing. The victim related to
me that there were four
suspects. I spoke with Dr.
Eaker, who advised me that*

he would give me a full
report shortly.

Just this one change reduced the length of the paragraph by 25% without any loss of information. And more significantly, this shorter version is probably 25% easier to write, easier to read, and easier to understand.

Enough? If you want to do the best possible job of communicating clearly, don't be afraid to say "I," "me," "my" and "mine." Your objectivity is going to be insured if you write a complete and accurate report. Your **credibility** is going to be enhanced if you write a readable, straightforward account of the things **you** did and saw and heard. What's more, you're going to reduce writing effort by simply saying "I," instead of "the undersigned officer."

Since there are some good reasons to be yourself, and no justifiable reasons for pretending you're not, I suggest you make that Change Number 1. It's easy.

□

WHO'S WHO?

What if all writers wrote about people the way most police officers do, preferring to call them by a classification and number rather than by name? Can you imagine, say, a history book where all the great explorers, presidents, and inventors were listed numerically on the first page and never called by name again in the book? Instead of reading about people like Marco Polo, Columbus, Lewis and Clark, Kit Carson, Washington, Jefferson, Lincoln, Edison, Bell, and Ford, we'd have stories like this:

> *During the administration of President No. 19, the West was being mapped by frontiersmen like Explorer No. 24 and Explorer No. 25. In Philadelphia, Inventor No. 18 was working on a sound recorder, while in*

> *Boston, Inventor No. 22 was serving as an apprentice to the man who would later become President No. 29.*

That wouldn't be too easy to follow, would it? You'd have to do what I do when I read your police reports: keep one finger on your place and turn back to the list of characters on page 1 to see who's who. Doing that constantly really slows down reading. I know from experience that it also slows down writing. So why write with labels rather than names? I don't know.

I do know one time when it's necessary. You have to use a label when you **don't know** a name. For instance, on a crime report where the suspects aren't known, I don't see any way around saying things like "Suspect No. 1 held the gun while Suspect No. 2 tied up EDWARDS." But you know EDWARDS' name, right? So why keep calling him "Victim No. 2"? By the time I get halfway through a report about labels, when I'm trying to find out what the **people** did and said, I'm usually about ready to send the report back for a rewrite.

The label problem comes in two varieties. Some officers list everybody on the face sheet of the report and then write the narrative part using **only** labels, and no names. How would you like to try reading things like this:

> *Reporting Party and Witness No. 2 confirmed what Witness No. 1 and Victim No.*

*1 had said, except that Witness No. 2
believed that Suspect No. 4 had worn the
red stocking mask, instead of Suspect No.
2, as reported by Witness No. 1, Victim No.
1, and Reporting Party. Witness No. 2 said
that Suspect No. 4 had picked up his
(Witness No.2) wallet and tossed it at him
(Witness No. 2), saying that they only
wanted Victim No. 1's and Victim No. 2's
property and would give his (Witness No.
2) back.*

The other kind of problem comes from officers who
use names in the body of the report but can't resist
the temptation to add bulk to the report by repeating
labels, too:

*Victim Bland found Victim Ross lying on
the sidewalk and administered first aid to
Victim Ross. Victim Bland related that
Witness Hendrix came by and called the
police. When we arived, Suspect Kinney
was found hiding in the laundry room and
Suspect Persinger was in the women's toilet.
Suspect Kinney and Suspect Persinger were
identified by Victim Bland and Victim
Ross.*

Once you have identified the people you're going
to be writing about, don't keep calling them by
labels—use their names. And don't keep repeating
words like "victim" and "witness"—you're only

throwing in filler, and slowing down everyone who has to read your reports.

An incidental problem of using labels and numbers where names are known is that the officer writing the report sometimes confuses himself and has "Victim No. 3" saying what "Victim No. 2" actually said. Sometimes the results are only hilarious; other times they may be fatal to our case by creating a basis for the impeachment of a prosecution witness by a "prior inconsistent statement."

□ □ □

The label "subject" ought to be thrown out entirely. Some officers just tack this one onto everyone who doesn't fit into one of the standard classifications, and then we get "Subject JACKSON," instead of simply "JACKSON." What does the word "subject" add? Verbiage. It **never** adds information, because a "subject" could be anyone. What can you tell from reading "Subject JACKSON" that you don't get from reading "JACKSON"? Nothing. It's just twice as much work for nothing.

And to take up even more time and space than necessary, some officers find ways to create two and three-word phrases around "subject" where a single word would have been better. For example, I often see officers write something like "young juvenile female subject." We have a word for this in plain

English—we call it a "girl." A "Caucasian adult male subject" is a "white man," and so on. See how easy it is to reduce writing effort?

There's also a drawback to the bad habit of saying "subject" when you really mean "man" or "woman." Suppose you have an armed robbery committed by a man and a woman and you write this statement:

> *When he hesitated, one of the subjects hit him with a gun barrel. The other subject was carrying a buck knife.*

Do your readers know who did what? Not the way you've written it. If you had never gotten into the bad habit of talking about "subjects," you'd have written the natural way, like you talk:

> *When he hesitated, the man hit him with a gun barrel. The woman was carrying a buck knife.*

Not only is this one more informative, it's also slightly less work.

Another problem with using the word "subject" in place of names or more factual descriptions is that it becomes pretty difficult to sneak in a normal use of "subject" without creating confusion:

> *The subject stated at this point the subject appeared dropped.*

I had to read that once twice.

My suggestions about labels are these:

(1) Don't **substitute** labels for names ("Victim No.2");

(2) Don't **add** labels to names ("Reporting Party EVANS");

(3) Don't **ever** use the label "subject."

And incidentally, everything I've said about labels for **people** also applies to labels for **things**—it's more informative, more factual, to say "apartment" than to say "residence" (which also covers houses, duplexes, hotel rooms, condominiums, mobile homes, etc.) And I recommend you throw out another of the police specials—"vehicle"—and replace it with more specific words like "car," "truck," "van," "motorcycle," and so on.

Before we leave the subject of labels (see—that's how "subject" is supposed to be used), here are a couple of final examples of how labels bog down reading and make you wonder after you've finished just what it is you've read:

EXAMPLES

Witness No. 1 PEREZ related that he and his victim brother-in-law Joe SOTO were playing pool. His victim brother-in-law SOTO was approached by numerous subjects at which time an argument started. As words were exchanged by his brother-in-law

victim SOTO and these same subjects, a
subject stepped forward with a cue stick and
struck his brother-in-law victim SOTO.
Witness No. 1 PEREZ then observed his
brother-in-law victim SOTO fall to the
ground. As Witness No. 1 PEREZ knelt
down to assist his brother-in-law victim
SOTO, he (Witness No. 1 PEREZ) observed
the assailant run away.

☐   ☐   ☐

She related that victim number four told
her about an incident involving her and the
subject. She said victim number two told
her the subject's son babysat victim number
four. The subject came over at bedtime
and, according to the information related to
her by victim number two which she had
been told by victim number four, the sub-
ject told her a bedtime story using the sub-
ject's private parts and victim number
four's private parts. Victim number two
related to her that the subject stuck his
private parts into victim number four's
private parts. This information she said was
related to victim number two by victim
number four, and she in turn told her.

Wouldn't it have been much easier to make sense
out of those two reports if the cops had forgotten
about labels and just used **names**? More than any
other occupational group I know of, police officers are

infatuated with labels. They're only stumbling blocks to easy reading. DON'T USE LABELS IF YOU CAN AVOID IT. Your reports will be more informative, less wordy, and easier to read.

□

WHODUNIT?

Here's a little murder mystery for you.

*Three men—Mr. Black, Mr. White and Mr.
Green—were invited to dinner and were
asked to bring a gift. A piece of jewelry was
brought, a fine book was given, and a bottle
of rare wine was presented to the host.
When the host tasted the wine, he died.
The wine had been poisoned by the guest
who had brought it.*

Whodunit—Mr. Black, Mr. White, or Mr. Green?
Can't tell, can you? That's what makes it a
"whodunit"—the writer tells you that certain things
"were done," but you have to figure out for yourself
who did them. If you had been told who brought the
wine, you'd know who killed the host. But you're

never going to be able to figure it out from the limited information you have. And now you know how people feel reading your reports when they come across something like this:

EXAMPLE

A search was conducted of the apartment. Six plastic syringes were located in a brown paper bag on the floor next to the sink. Two more syringes were found beneath the mattress and two burnt bottle caps were located in the top left-hand dresser drawer. All three subjects were then transported to the station, where they were advised of their rights. After waivers were taken, the subjects were interviewed and admitted injecting heroin in the apartment. Subject Philips was given a urine sample and the other subjects Milne and Bybee were given blood samples. All subjects were evaluated for being under the influence of opiates and it was determined they were.

If only **one** officer had been listed on this report, maybe it would be safe to assume he was the one who did everything that the report says "was done." The problem was that the report listed **five** police officers, all of whom were apparently involved in these various activities. The case came to trial five months after the arrest. Do you suppose the officers could remember

who did **what?** They could not. Could they tell from reviewing the report? They could not. So could each officer testify as to those things he did? No.

Look at what a "whodunit" that portion of the report is (the rest wasn't much better):

"A search **was conducted** . . ." (**Who** conducted it?)

". . . syringes **were located** . . ." (**Who** found them?)

". . . the subjects **were transported** . . ." (**Who** took them?)

". . . **were advised** of their rights." (**Who** advised them?)

". . . waivers **were taken** . . ." (**Who** took them?)

". . . subjects **were interviewed** . . ." (Whodunit?)

". . . blood and urine samples **were taken.**" (Whodunit?)

". . . subjects **were evaluated** . . ." (Whodunit?)

". . . it **was determined** . . ." (Whodunit?)

You're not supposed to be writing a whodunit! If the cop who wrote that piece of mystery had told me **who** found each item of evidence, I'd know who to put on the stand to get it introduced. If he had told me **who** got the **Miranda** waiver, I'd know who could testify about that. And so on. But he didn't. The only people who got any help from that report were the three hypes and their attorney.

I can only guess as to who did what, but it should

have been written this way:

> *All five of us searched the apartment. Officer COLTER found six plastic syringes in a brown paper bag on the floor next to the sink. Officer DEHAVEN found two syringes under the mattress and two burnt bottle caps in the top left-hand dresser drawer. Officer NEWBURG and I took the arrested men to the station. (Etc.)*

"Whodunit" questions can be answered two different ways:

1. First describe **what was done**, then tell **who did it.**

or

2. First tell **who did it**, then tell **what was done.**

Does it matter which way you do it? Yes! Look:

EXAMPLES

1. *The gun was found by KENDALL.*
2. *KENDALL found the gun.*

What's the difference? The first sentence is 50% longer than the second, and yet both sentences tell exactly the same information! Why do 1½ times the work you need to? Work smarter, not harder. The shortest, easiest way to write is to name the actor **first,** and **then** tell what action he took.

Not only is this method less work, it's also the only

sure way to avoid writing "whodunits." It forces you to put in the "who" of the "whodunit" before you can say anything else; the longer method of writing allows you to become careless and create a whodunit.

If you're in the habit of writing like this:

A radio dispatch was monitored by Officer Lee, you may forget to put the **who did it** on the end, and you wind up with this:

A radio dispatch was monitored.

That's a "whodunit," and it can come back to haunt you months later when you're trying to recall the facts for the jury, and all you've got to assist a hazy memory is an even hazier report full of "whodunits." You won't have that problem if you always put the **who did it** part first, and then tell **what was done.**

There you have two good reasons (less work and more facts) for putting the actor first. Unless you know of some better reasons for doing things the backward, harder, longer, riskier way, I suggest you add this rule of writing to all those rules you memorized in school (i before e, etc.): **who** before **what.**

Another thing to remember to avoid writing a "whodunit" is that I can't call "it" as a witness; "it" can't testify.

Look:

EXAMPLES

ARTIFICIAL: *It was determined that the*

property belonged to Katz.

That's not only a "whodunit," it's also a "howdunit." (**Who** determined? **How** was it determined?)

NATURAL: *Katz told me the property was his.*

      □   □   □

ARTIFICIAL: *It was learned that the car was going south on Grand.*

NATURAL: *The dispatcher said the car was going south on Grand.*

      □   □   □

ARTIFICIAL: *It was concluded that a warrant should be sought.*

NATURAL: *We decided to seek a warrant.*

      □   □   □

ARTIFICIAL: *It was ascertained that the powder was 4% heroin.*

NATURAL: *The lab report said the powder was 4% heroin.*

      □   □   □

ARTIFICIAL: *It* was felt that he was drunk.

NATURAL: *I felt he was drunk.*

      □   □   □

See how the natural versions—which are usually less work—tell **more information?** They tell **who** did things, and **how** things were done. If you want to communicate as much information as possible, don't start a sentence by saying: "**It** was determined that . . ." Instead, tell your readers **who** did it, and **how.** Leave the whodunits to Ellery Queen.

SEARCH OF G.L. MARTIN'S CAR SHOWING APPROX LOCATIONS OF ITEMS SEIZED BY OFFICERS TANAKA AND ROSS. SKETCH BY TANAKA #113 No SCALE.

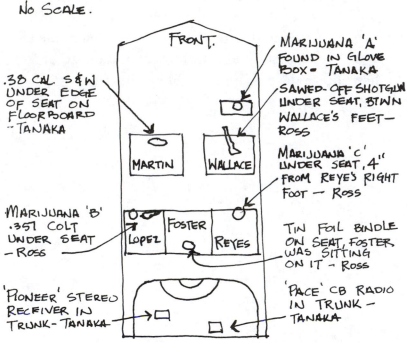

A sketch like this is worth a lot of words in a report. It enables me to see at a glance which defendants can be charged with which counts of illegal possession. And it enables you to recall **who** found **what where**, near **whom**, even if you don't get called to testify for several months. Sketches can be used for auto and house searches, traffic collisions, and any serious crime scene.

WORDS AND PHRASES

You may not have realized that "gobbledygook" is a real word, but it is. This is how my dictionary defines it:

> *"Wordy and generally unintelligible jargon; inflated, involved and obscure verbiage characteristic of the pronouncements of officialdom."*

Gobbledygook is the language that lawyers, government bureaucrats, and—guess who?—**police officers** write in. It's the language that's responsible for those ridiculous quotations I gave you from the corporations code. It's the language that makes it nearly impossible for a person to do his own income tax returns. And it's the language that causes a cop to write:

> *"This officer interrupted this officer's forward acceleration, immediately bringing this officer to a status of zero acceleration,"*

when all he means is

> *"I stopped."*

Some people are in love with gobbledygook. But then some people go out of their way to over-complicate everything, just for the sake of making work. I've never seen the police department that had the budget or the personnel to do a lot of unnecessary work. So I suggest you stay away from words and phrases that make gobbledygook out of your writing.

Some people feel betrayed when I tell them to simplify their writing—to forget about using all those "buzz words" and "catch phrases" that only a veteran cop knows how to throw around. And some people feel insulted when I poke fun at their college vocabulary and ask them to write in plain old every-day conversational English. After all, they've cultivated that big vocabulary very carefully, ever since the high school teacher made them memorize a list of the 300 least-used words in the language. They're proud of themselves when they see a way to work "rectify" and "acrimonious" into a report about a stolen CB.

I know the feeling. I once went to the trouble of memorizing the meaning of such words as "magniloquent" and "pusillanimous." But I'm willing to admit to myself now that I didn't learn those words to communicate; I learned them to impress. I never use them anymore. They still sit on the bench in my **reading** vocabulary, along with "iconoclastic," "loquacious," "rusticate," "taciturn," and "vapid," but I make a point of not using them for **speaking** or **writing**. And don't get me wrong—I'm not saying there's anything wrong with **knowing** a lot of uncommon words. I'm merely suggesting you don't put them in places where people are going to trip over them.

When you were getting all that advice all your life about how important the giant vocabulary was, I think it should have been put to you this way. Communication is a two-way street. Half of it is **understanding** what you hear and read; the other half is **being understood** in what you say and write. For the first half, it's helpful to be familiar with as many words and technical phrases as possible. Then, no matter what level of speech you're listening to or what kind of material you're reading, you can get the other person's information and make it yours.

But for the second half, you've got to do your talking and writing with the most commonly-used words you can find, or you run the risk of failing to communicate your information to the audience you're talking or writing to. When you write a police report, keep in mind that it may be read by other cops, prosecutors and other attorneys, judges, probation and parole officers, jurors, the parties, the witnesses, insurance adjustors, statisticians, and others I probably don't even know about. Your objective in writing should be to communicate the same information to as many of your readers as possible. That means using words and phrases that most people are familiar with, and avoiding language that leaves some or all of your readers wondering what you mean.

Here's an example. Suppose the number beside each of the words listed below is the percentage of your readers who will understand a sentence where you use that word:

recrement *2%*
supererogation *3%*
superfluity *10%*
surplusage *25%*
overabundance *85%*
excess *95%*
too much *100%*

All of those words mean more or less the same thing. But if you write with words like "recrement" and "supererogation," you aren't going to accomplish your objective of communicating. The more obscure your words are, the more of your audience you're going to lose; the more familiar your words are, the more successful you're going to be at communicating (and the easier it's going to be to read and rely on your reports).

So while I don't blame you if you want to know what "recrement" means when you hear it or read it, I'd think you were crazy if you used it in everyday speaking or in a police report. I'd know you were only trying to sound impressive, and so would everyone else who read your report. Trying to sound impressive is not a legitimate goal of a police report (nor, for that matter, of any other kind of writing I can think of). You don't have to be ashamed of using everyday words like "too much."

By the way, notice that I'm not necessarily contrasting **long** words and **short** words, but **unfamiliar** and **familiar** words. "Pule" is a short word, but it's unfamiliar. Don't use it. "Cooperation" is relatively long, but just about everybody understands it. Go ahead and use it. Don't worry so much about the **length** of words; just try to talk in common language that will communicate your information clearly to the maximum number of readers.

Do you suppose that for some strange reason police officers actually prefer to do things the difficult way? I doubt it. But I'm hard-pressed to explain why I keep seeing so many reports where the officer seemingly went out of his way to make extra work out of everything he wrote.

Below are examples of sentences taken from gobbledygook reports, followed by sentences that say the same thing in plain talk. Notice that the plain-talk sentences are not only clearer, but also much shorter in almost every case (which means it took **less work** to say the same things **better**).

EXAMPLES

ARTIFICIAL: *They became engaged in an argument.*

NATURAL: *They argued.*

□   □   □

ARTIFICIAL: *The bandages were clean and appeared new in appearance.*

NATURAL: *The bandages were clean and appeared new.*

□   □   □

ARTIFICIAL: *I effected a carstop and alighted from the police vehicle.*

NATURAL: *I made a carstop and got out of the police car.*

□   □   □

ARTIFICIAL: *At this point, using my police baton, I threw it at his feet.*

NATURAL: *Then I threw my baton at his feet.*

□   □   □

ARTIFICIAL: *I was in the vicinity of Lincoln Park involving myself in an area search for the unknown subjects.*

NATURAL: *I was searching for the suspects around Lincoln Park.*

☐ ☐ ☐

ARTIFICIAL: *I submitted the check for the purpose of handwriting analysis.*

NATURAL: *I turned in the check for handwriting analysis.*

☐ ☐ ☐

ARTIFICIAL: *The anticipated response to the present date has been none.*

NATURAL: *There has been no response.*

☐ ☐ ☐

ARTIFICIAL: *I telephonically contacted him at his place of residence.*

NATURAL: *I phoned him at his home.*

☐ ☐ ☐

ARTIFICIAL: *We responded to the area of the intersection of 4th and Main.*

NATURAL: *We drove to 4th and Main.*

☐ ☐ ☐

ARTIFICIAL: *I requested of her that she respond to my location at the Dairy Mart.*

NATURAL: *I asked her to come to the Dairy Mart.*

☐   ☐   ☐

ARTIFICIAL: *I proceeded to make an examination of the skid marks.*

NATURAL: *I examined the skid marks.*

☐   ☐   ☐

ARTIFICIAL: *I proceeded to conduct an interview with the witnesses.*

NATURAL: *I interviewed the witnesses.*

☐   ☐   ☐

ARTIFICIAL: *Potts proceeded to strike him about the face and head with closed fists.*

NATURAL: *Potts hit him in the face and head with his fists.*

(As far as I know, there's no such thing as an ''open'' fist.)

☐   ☐   ☐

ARTIFICIAL: *We then proceeded to the upstairs area.*

NATURAL: *Then we went upstairs.*

☐   ☐   ☐

ARTIFICIAL: *I observed there to be a*

number of pry marks on the windwing.

NATURAL: *I saw several pry marks on the windwing.*

□   □   □

ARTIFICIAL: *We were making an effort to eliminate his flight.*

NATURAL: *We were trying to stop him.*

□   □   □

ARTIFICIAL: *I inquired of him as to whether or not he would converse with me regarding the property.*

NATURAL: *I asked him if he would talk to me about the property.*

□   □   □

ARTIFICIAL: *A verbal altercation ensued.*

NATURAL: *An argument followed.*

□   □   □

ARTIFICIAL: *We had occasion to hold a meeting.*

NATURAL: *We met.*

□   □   □

ARTIFICIAL: *I was attempting to ascertain his precise direction of travel.*

NATURAL: *I was trying to find out which way he went.*

ARTIFICIAL: *There was a loss to the owners in the amount of $212.*

NATURAL: *The owners lost $212.*

☐ ☐ ☐

ARTIFICIAL: *I had a suspicion that she was the one.*

NATURAL: *I suspected her.*

☐ ☐ ☐

ARTIFICIAL: *Subsequent to our making arrangements for an additional purchase, we delivered the powder to the crime lab for the purpose of analysis.*

NATURAL: *After we arranged another purchase, we took the powder to the crime lab for analysis.*

☐ ☐ ☐

ARTIFICIAL: *It was further described as being round in shape.*

NATURAL: *It was round.*

☐ ☐ ☐

ARTIFICIAL: *The car I was following was a 1964 Buick, blue in color.*

NATURAL: *I was following a blue 1964 Buick.*

ARTIFICIAL: *The total length of the locked-wheel skid was 72 feet in length.*

NATURAL: *The locked-wheel skid was 72 feet long.*

☐　　☐　　☐

ARTIFICIAL: *Investigator Lindsey questioned him in reference to the rifle, due to the fact that we had knowledge that a rifle had in fact been carried by one of the suspects during the commission of the robbery.*

NATURAL: *Investigator Lindsey questioned him about the rifle because we knew one suspect had carried a rifle during the robbery.*

☐　　☐　　☐

ARTIFICIAL: *At that point in time we were not actually in the possession of any description; however, at the present time we do have a description.*

NATURAL: *We had no description then; now we do.*

☐　　☐　　☐

ARTIFICIAL: *Both officers maintained visual surveillance of the residence for a period of 45 minutes.*

NATURAL: *Both officers watched the house for 45 minutes.*

☐ ☐ ☐

ARTIFICIAL: *REIDY related that HART informed him in regard to the physical altercation.*

NATURAL: *REIDY said HART told him about the fight.*

☐ ☐ ☐

ARTIFICIAL: *A bystander initiated a conversation with me reference the accident.*

NATURAL: *A bystander started talking to me about the accident.*

☐ ☐ ☐

ARTIFICIAL: *I hurriedly responded to the rear portion of the yard area where I proceeded to establish surveillance in terms of the door and windows.*

NATURAL: *I ran to the back yard and watched the door and windows.*

☐ ☐ ☐

ARTIFICIAL: *Some person inside, unknown who, extinguished all interior sources of artificial illumination.*

NATURAL: *Someone inside turned out the lights.*

☐   ☐   ☐

ARTIFICIAL: *As I descended the driveway area leading to the subterranean parking lot, I observed adjacent to the elevator area a subject lying on the ground clutching his side area with his hands.*

NATURAL: *As I went down the driveway to the underground parking lot, I saw a man lying near the elevator, holding his side.*

☐   ☐   ☐

ARTIFICIAL: *Assigned officers advised the informant/victim GLOVER to respond to the Sheriff's Department during the next day time period to have photographs taken of the area which has sustained the injuries inflicted upon him.*

NATURAL: *We told GLOVER to go to the Sheriff's Department the next day to have pictures taken of his injuries.*

☐　　☐　　☐

ARTIFICIAL: *I denoted an odor of alcohol emitting from her breath.*

NATURAL: *I smelled alcohol on her breath.*

☐　　☐　　☐

ARTIFICIAL: *During the altercation, HALL attempted to subject JOINER to the application of a choking procedure.*

NATURAL: *During the fight, HALL tried to choke JOINER.*

☐　　☐　　☐

Now that we've gone through all those examples, it's easy to make a list of words and phrases that add nothing to a report but extra work for the writer and the reader. Plain-talk substitutes are also easy to list. This chart isn't complete, of course, but there's enough here to give you a good idea of how to cut down on work and improve readability.

When you're tempted to use these wordy, **artificial expressions** . . .	Try using these better, more **natural** ones, instead:
made an effort made an attempt endeavored attempted	tried
maintained surveillance over kept under observation visually monitored	watched
related stated verbalized articulated	said
informed advised indicated communicated verbally	told
initiated instigated commenced inaugurated originated	began
alighted from exited dismounted	got out

ARTIFICIAL	NATURAL
telephonically contacted reached via landline contacted by telephone	phoned
responded proceeded	went, walked, drove, etc.
placed under arrest effected an arrest on	arrested
was new in appearance	appeared new
was cold to the touch	felt cold
was sour to the taste	tasted sour
altercation mutual combat physical confrontation exchange of physi- cal blows	fight
verbal altercation verbal dispute verbal confrontation	argument
at this point at this time at which time at which point in time	then
as of this date as of this time as of the present time	yet
red in color	red

ARTIFICIAL	NATURAL
requested inquired queried	asked
visually perceived visually noticed observed viewed	saw
was in the possession of had possession of	had
presently currently at the present at the present time at this time	now
prior to previous to in advance of	before
subsequent to	after
for the purpose of	for
for the reason that in order that	so
in reference to reference in regard to regarding on the subject of	about
round in shape	round

ARTIFICIAL	NATURAL
in order to with the intention of with the objective to	to
due to the fact that considering that as a result of the fact that in view of the fact that in light of the fact that	because, since
6' in height 2' in width 3' in length 8'' in depth	6' high, 6' tall 2' wide 3' long 8'' deep

Reducing work and improving clarity aren't the only things you guarantee when you use common vocabulary instead of the pompous expressions that have become almost "standard" police jargon. You'll also be making sure that you don't misuse a word you **thought** you knew the meaning of; I've seen cops get laughed right off the witness stand when smart-aleck defense lawyers read back sentences from reports that weren't really meant to be funny.

Here's what happens when you abandon the everyday vocabulary you're used to using and start trying to sound impressive:

EXAMPLES

ARTIFICIAL: *I proceeded back to the location of the damaged vechicle to ascertain exactly what was expiring.*

(This officer obviously **meant** to say "transpiring;" he never would have had a problem if he'd just stuck to plain talk.)

NATURAL: *I went back to the damaged car to find out what was happening.*

□   □   □

ARTIFICIAL: *Before placing him into the unit, assigned officer made a courtesy search of his clothing.*

(The word he was trying for was "cursory;" I wouldn't use it.)

NATURAL: *I patted him down before I put him in the police car.*

□   □   □

ARTIFICIAL: *I attempted to question him on the pertinence of his identity and his place of abord.*

(Can you picture the cop saying to someone: "What's the pertinence of your identity?")

IT'S NOT ALWAYS YOUR FAULT . . .

you dictated. . .

"I called for the paramedics . . ."

"I got the rain gear out of my car . . ."

"I called for a tow truck . . ."

"The criminalist will be taking ac-
crued vacation . . ."

"He was crouched down behind the van . . ."

but your secretary typed. . .

"I called for the pair of medics .. ."

"I got the reindeer out of my car . .."

"I called for a toe truck . . ."

"The criminalist will be taking a crude vacation . . ."

"He was crotched down behind the van. . ."

NATURAL: *I asked him his name and address.*

☐   ☐   ☐

ARTIFICIAL: *LOZANO reinnervated the same information as BAILEY had related.*

(You can tell this officer doesn't normally use the word "reiterated." He shouldn't have tried using it in a report.)

NATURAL: *LOZANO said the same thing as BAILEY.*

☐   ☐   ☐

Here are some "one-liners:"

I observed the suspect setted on the fence.

☐   ☐   ☐

The driver exited himself as JOEY RODRIGUEZ.

☐   ☐   ☐

I observed an inmate pronced on the upper bunk.

☐   ☐   ☐

The victim substained bruises on both buttocks.

☐   ☐   ☐

She, however, indicated that no bruises exited.

☐   ☐   ☐

He asked me if I had monitored the loud noise with any kind of machine to check the decimals.

☐   ☐   ☐

We set up a photo line-up for the purpose of illumination of RODGERS as a suspect.

☐   ☐   ☐

And this one got a lot of laughs from the jury and spectators:

Having prior knowledge of the prostitution problem in the area of 400 N. Broadway, Investigator Donovan and I went to that area in order to elevate the problem.

☐   ☐   ☐

Obviously, if you don't know the difference between "elevate" and "alleviate," you don't have any business using either one. And remember that if you aren't too sure what a word means, your reader probably isn't either. So you're either going to fail to communicate altogether, or you're going to say something you didn't really mean. Aren't those good enough reasons to stick to your normal, everyday vocabulary?

If you want to take time for a little practical exercise, get out your pencil and paper and rewrite this passage from a gobbledygook report.

As Reporting Officer deployed the beam from his flashlight to illumine the interior

> *area of the vehicle, Reporting Officer was able to visually observe that both male subjects had their various articles of clothing, including their underwear, below the area of their knees, thus being in fact nude from the waist down. Reporting Officer then requested both subjects to assume an erect position and place their hands in a position of plain view from whence they might be observed by Reporting Officer. As the two subjects complied to my request, Reporting Officer noticed that both subjects at this particular time had their penises in an erective condition.*

And for another kind of comparison, here's an account of a traffic accident written by a policeman, followed by the handwritten version of the citizen. **OFFICER:**

> *Driver No. 1 related that his vehicle was northbound in the center lane. He stated that he felt another vehicle strike the rear of his vehicle, whereupon Driver No. 1 indicated for Driver No. 2 to proceed to the right edge of the roadway. Driver No. 1 related that Driver No. 2 then laughed and made an obscene gesture by extending his middle finger, and proceeded to drive away from the scene of the accident. At this time, Driver No. 1 recorded the license number of vehicle No. 2, that being 843 ASA.*

CITIZEN:

> *I was going north in the center lane when I felt someone hit my rear end. I waved the man over to the right lane; he laughed and gave me the finger, so I took his license #843 ASA.*

If I hadn't labeled those two versions, would you still have been able to tell which one the cop wrote, and which one the citizen wrote? Sure you would. How could you tell? Because one is written in common, easy-to-understand straight talk; the other is written in typical police gobbledygook. That's how different police reporting is—you can easily tell it apart from plain English.

And just as you wouldn't write in English to someone whose native language is Russian and expect him to understand you, you shouldn't expect **anyone** to understand what you write in gobbledygook, because that's **nobody's** native language. It's just a contrived language that different groups of officials have made up to make themselves sound more educated and professional than the rest of us. Instead, of course, they only sound more pompous and insincere. I recommend against gobbledygook in your reports. If you know a good reason for hanging on to it, I'd sure like to hear it—I haven't heard one yet.

□

SAY WHAT
YOU MEAN

There are a lot of official grammar rules to tell you what order to put your words in to make the sentences mean what you want to say. The trouble with most of those rules is that they themselves use an English professor's technical jargon, and if you've never been able to keep the terminology memorized, the rules don't have any meaning. If you're like most people, you had just a good enough grasp of terms like "misplaced modifier" and "pronoun-antecedent agreement" to get you through a test, and then the niceties of grammar slipped away with all the dates you memorized for history exams and the useless facts you once knew about the geography of Ecuador.

In spite of this reality, I notice that people who teach report-writing classes and those who write books on the subject are still trying to get you to memorize the rules about sentence construction. That's fine if you can do it—there's nothing wrong with being able to tell whether a pronominal subject of an infinitive clause is in the nominative or the objective case. The fact is, though, that if you didn't learn such things in the 6th grade, or the 8th, or the 10th or 12th, you're probably never going to.

What you **can** do very easily is to read what you've written (if you dictate your reports by phone, ask your supervisor for an opportunity to review the typed product). When you read through your reports, ask yourself whether there are two ways of reading what you've written; if so, how could you have written it so that there would only be one?

Usually, rearranging word order will help remove ambiguities.

EXAMPLES

He was 5'6'', 175 lbs., long dark hair, and wearing a heavy green overcoat with sideburns.

Did the officer intend to say that the overcoat had sideburns? Of course not. And he doesn't have to know any rules about ''misplaced modifiers'' to correct it. If he simply read the sentence and asked himself if he had said what he meant, he'd have no trouble rearranging the sentence correctly:

> *He was 5'6'', 175 lbs., long dark hair, sideburns, and wearing a heavy green overcoat.*

A grammarian can tell you that this revision isn't correct, either. Don't worry about it. This revision communicates just as well as this longer, ''parallel'' version:

> *He was 5'6'' and 175 lbs., had sideburns and long dark hair, and wore a heavy green overcoat.*

''Parallelism'' is a nicety. You can pick up niceties along the way, but concentrate **first** on accurate communication.

☐   ☐   ☐

> *I was advised by radio that the vehicle had committed a theft at Sears.*

A vehicle can't commit a theft, of course. Say what you mean:

> *I heard by radio that the car was driven from Sears by the shoplifter.*

☐   ☐   ☐

> *While enroute to the station, Subject COLLINS unlocked the door to the patrol unit and attempted to exit at approximately 40 m.p.h.*

What was going 40 m.p.h.—Collins or the car? Say what you mean:

> *We were enroute to the station at about 40 m.p.h. when COLLINS unlocked the car door and tried to jump out.*

☐   ☐   ☐

> *BERRY was unable to satisfactorily perform the field sobriety test. Sgt. Decker arrived and another test was given. His performance was the same.*

Was Sgt. Decker drunk? Say what you mean:

> *BERRY failed the first field sobriety test, and he failed a second test I gave him after Sgt. Decker came.*

☐   ☐   ☐

> *Upon arrival of Sgt. Ross at the location, based on the above objective symptoms, he was advised he was being placed under arrest for addiction to heroin.*

Is Sgt. Ross a hype? Say what you mean:

> *After Sgt. Ross came, I told ESPINOSA he was under arrest for heroin addiction.*

☐   ☐   ☐

> *He kept yelling profanity and calling us all the deputies names.*

Oh yeah?

☐   ☐   ☐

Both subjects then walked over to the display rack containing the white men's polo t-shirts.

Do only **white** men wear these shirts? Say what you mean:

Both men walked over to the display rack where the men's white polo t-shirts were.

☐   ☐   ☐

He reached into the glove compartment and withdrew a black man's wallet.

Same problem. Try this:

He reached into the glove compartment and took out a man's black wallet.

☐   ☐   ☐

The two driver's licenses had three different similarities.

. . .?

☐   ☐   ☐

If you can't get the sentence to say what you mean by rearranging the words, maybe you're trying to cram too many things into a single sentence. Break it down into two or more shorter sentences.

EXAMPLE

Officer Berg was able to locate the injection marks, see his narcotic evaluation report, under magnification and light.

Are we supposed to look at the report under magnification? That's what it says. But it's easy to correct. Break it into two sentences:

> *Officer Berg found the injection marks under magnification and light. See his narcotic evaluation report.*

☐   ☐   ☐

Another problem with long sentences is that they can get you so bogged down that you wind up not finishing what you started out to say.

EXAMPLE

> *While investigating a robbery, in which the victim ANDREWS, had observed a subject threaten him with a knife, in which property was removed from his person.*

You get the feeling, don't you, that this officer was going to tell us something that happened while he was investigating? But he never got to it—he got sidetracked by his own wordiness.

If you get too preoccupied with gobbledygook, you may leave out things you meant to say and instead say something absurd.

EXAMPLES

> *Assigned officers responded to that area and did not observe the vehicle but did make contact with his sister, Mary URIE.*

Is Mary Urie the sister of a vehicle? Say what you mean:

> *We went there and didn't see the car, but we talked to Mary URIE. She is the driver's sister.*

□   □   □

> *While they were trying them on one pair of their old shoes came up missing, however, loitering in the shoe department for a lengthy time period the old pair of shoes was returned to the suspect's feet.*

That's not the clearest piece of writing in the world. Say what you mean:

> *While the suspects were trying on new shoes, one pair of their old ones disappeared. The suspects loitered in the shoe department for awhile. Later, the manager noticed that the suspect had his old shoes on again.*

□   □   □

If you get into trouble by saying "he" or "him" after you've mentioned two different men in the same sentence, you don't have to sit down and memorize rules about "pronoun agreement." Just read your sentence; if it doesn't say what you mean, and if rearranging or breaking it into shorter sentences won't help, simply substitute **names** for "he" and "him" wherever you need to for clarity.

EXAMPLE

> *FLORES advised that ORTIZ began de-*
> *manding to see his daughter and he began*
> *denying him that privilege. He then began*
> *stating that he had fired a shot at him.*

Was Flores trying to see his own daughter or Ortiz'
daughter? Who fired at whom? Throw out some of
the ''he's'' and ''him's'', shorten the sentences, and
plug in names:

> *FLORES said ORTIZ demanded to see*
> *FLORES' daughter. FLORES wouldn't let*
> *him. FLORES said ORTIZ then fired a*
> *shot at him.*

(Don't waste words by using **both** the names and the
pronoun: "He (FLORES) said that he (ORTIZ) . . ."
If you're going to have to use names to make your
meaning clear, drop the ''he.'')

If you want to go to night school and take a basic
grammar course, that's fine—most people can use a
periodic brush-up. Just don't confuse **purposes**. The
purpose of a composition written in proper English is
often just to demonstrate a mastery of the rules. The
purpose of your reports (to communicate information) doesn't necessarily require you to follow the
rules. For example, if you worry too much about such
things as dangling prepositions and split infinitives,
you could wind up writing sentences that sound too
artificial to be taken seriously.

EXAMPLES

> *I didn't know who else to turn to.*

That sentence has two grammatical errors in it, and a contraction. But if you followed all the formal writing rules, look how silly it would sound:

> *I did not know to whom else to turn.*

Here's another one:

> *He refused to even listen or to really try to cooperate.*

Two split infinitives. But if you used ''correct'' grammar:

> *He refused even to listen or really to try to cooperate.*

☐   ☐   ☐

The point isn't that it's bad to know and use the official rules of grammar—in most cases, you'll write better if you've learned the basics and an occasional nicety. The point is that you shouldn't get boxed in by the rules to the extent that your ability to communicate suffers, and you don't have to feel that the only way you can write well is by memorizing the terminology, rules, and exceptions from an English text. If you say what you mean, the same way you talk, you're going to come out ahead. It's not unusual for someone to try so hard to sound grammatical that he pulls boners like these (all of these examples are grammatically incorrect):

EXAMPLES

- *That depends on whom has it.*
- *He threw the bottle in the direction of my partner and I.*
- *JOHNSON was transported by myself.*
- *I released it to whomever filed the claim.*
- *The parents feel they are losing control, which Tommy has been staying out at night, which they are afraid he may be using dope.*

Chances are, if the cops who wrote those sentences had just put it down the way they normally **talk**, everything would have come out fine. It's the same old story: trying to impress and reaching for some artificial word or expression causes only work and confusion (if not comedy). Be natural. Simply say what you mean, and read your own writing whenever you can to make sure it **does** say only what you mean.

☐

LIVING WITH YOUR REPORT

When you go out to the crime scene, you see things. You question people and **hear** what they say. Maybe you **smell** or **taste** something. Maybe you put your hands on an object, or you search a suspect: you **feel** things. And all the time you're there, you're **doing** things.

Now all you have to do when it's all over is to write it down so that everyone reading your report will get an accurate picture of what's in your head when you sit down to do the report. Difficult? Not really. The key to painting an accurate picture of the crime scene and the important things that happened there is to set things down in proper order, in plain language, and to tell the reader the **source** of your information.

EXAMPLE

> *A third passenger managed to crawl out of the overturned car.*

This sentence was written by an officer investigating a fatal traffic accident. What was the **source** of his information? (Don't worry about this sentence being out of context—the context it came from wasn't any help.) You can't tell, can you, whether this was something the officer **saw** while he was there, or something someone **told** him had happened?

Depending on the source, he should have written one of these:

> *I saw a third passenger crawl out of the over-turned car.*

or,

> *DOLAN told me he saw a third passenger crawl out of the overturned car.*

Why does it matter whether or not your report shows the sources of the various things you record? It matters because without **sources**, your report doesn't paint an accurate and complete picture for the readers. It matters because without **sources**, you and I are going to be unable to live with your report very well. If we can't live with it very well, the defendant can live with it just fine, and all of your good police work is down the drain.

Take the example above. There was a problem in the case proving which of three people was driving the car that overturned, killing one of the occupants (all three had blood alcohol levels above .15). When it was time for me to subpena witnesses for the preliminary hearing, I couldn't tell from the report whether I needed only the officer, or only Dolan, or both, or any one of half a dozen other witnesses who might have told the officer about the guy who crawled out. What's worse, when I called and asked the cop, he said: "No, I didn't see that . . . somebody just told me . . . Who? . . .Uh, well . . . if it's not in my report, I don't know who it was."

"IF IT'S NOT IN MY REPORT, I DON'T KNOW." In most cases, you're always going to be in that position. You know and I know that it often takes anywhere from two months to two years to get a case to trial. In the meantime, you've made dozens—or maybe even hundreds—of similar arrests. When you're called to the witness stand to testify to details of a crime or arrest that took place several months earlier, you're going to remember some things, but you're going to have to depend on your report to help you recall particular details accurately. If they're not in your report, and if the jury keeps hearing you say "I don't know" to questions you should be able to answer, your testimony isn't going to help anybody but the defendant. He can live with your report, but you can't. It should be the other way around.

There are two kinds of things that make it hard for you to live with a report: things you've said, and things you haven't. If you write the things you say in vague, general, conclusionary, gobbledygook language, you're not going to be able to live with the ambiguities and the imprecision. If you fail to report things you should (like the **source** of every fact and observation), you're not going to be able to live with the omissions—either you're going to be repeating ''I don't know'' to every other question, or you're going to find yourself on the losing end of this familiar exchange with a defense attorney when you start testifying to things that aren't in your report.

Q: *Now, Officer, you wrote a report about this arrest, didn't you?*

A: *Yes, sir.*

Q: *And wasn't the purpose of that report to record all the important information about the case?*

A: *Yes, I guess so.*

Q: *I take it, Officer, that these events were clearer in your mind when you wrote the report than they are now, some six months later, right?*

A: *That's right.*

Q: *Did you deliberately leave out any significant details when you wrote the report?*

A: *No, sir.*

Q: *Don't you think it's significant to know which one of these men hit the other one first?*

A: *Yes.*

Q: *And it's your testimony today that you saw SHARP hit PETERS first, is that right?*

A: *That's right.*

Q: *Now Officer, did you put that in your report?*

A: *No, I guess I didn't.*

Q: *Would you care to explain to the jury, Officer, whether you left that out of your report because you didn't consider it significant at the time, or whether it's something you've just now recalled, six months later?*

Once you've gone this far down the path, any answer you give is going to hurt your credibility. Anything that hurts your credibility is going to help the defendant. (The answers the cop gave above are the ones I always hear; several of these answers are **dead wrong** and get you into witness-stand quicksand. In a few minutes, I'll suggest a better way to handle this trap.)

As I said, it isn't just things you **fail** to say that can make it difficult to live with your report down the line. It's every sloppy sentence of every gobbledygook paragraph you write. Look:

Q: *Now, Officer, your report says this: "Undersigned Detective received information to the effect that a subject by the name of J.L. Belt resided at the residence of 939 East 17th Street on February 6, 1978." Is that right?*

A: *Yes, sir.*

Q: *Just who was the "undersigned detective"?*

A: *That was me.*

Q: *How did you "receive information"—was that in person, by mail, by phone, by radio, or by E.S.P.?*

A: *I don't recall now, sir . . . it's been approximately five months since I wrote that. I'm sure it wasn't by E.S.P.*

Q: *Who did the "information" come from?*

A: *It was either an informant or another officer.*

Q: *In other words, you don't remember?*

A: *I don't remember.*

Q: *You've written that it was "to the effect that" such and such. Was that precisely what you were informed, or were you told something else from which you drew a conclusion that such and such was the* *case? In other words, do you remember what you were told?*

A: *Not exactly, no.*

Q: *This "subject" J.L. Belt—was this a "male subject" or a "female subject"?*

A: *As I recall, I believe it was a male subject.*

Q: *Are you sure it wasn't a woman?*

A: *No, sir . . . it's been five months . . . it could have been a female . . . my report just says "subject."*

Q: *In other words, you don't know whether that was a man or a woman, do you?*

A: *No.*

Q: *Now, Officer, you mentioned a "residence" at such and such an address. Was that a house, or an apartment, or a condominium, or a mobile home, or a duplex, or just what?*

A: *As I recall, I think it was a regular house.*

Q: *Are you sure about that?*

A: *No.*

Q: *Now you mention the date February 6, 1978. Was that the date when J.L. Belt was living there on 17th Street?*

A: *No, sir. That was the date when I received the information. I had this information before I requested the search warrant.*

Q: *Officer, read that sentence from your*

> *report to yourself . . . Now, according to*
> *your report, was February 6 the date when*
> *you got the information, or the date when*
> *Belt was supposed to have been living on*
> *17th?*

A: *Well, the way my report reads, I guess it*
looks like the date when Belt was living
there . . . but what I meant to say
was. ..

Q: *Thank you, Officer, I believe that'll do.*
Let's move on to the next thing in your
report.

See? You see how tough it can be to live with every single sentence of a poorly-written report? Can you imagine how your credibility will have suffered by the time the jury has watched you squirm around ten or twenty such sentences?

There's no changing your report once you've finished it and filed it. Once it becomes subject to discovery by the defense, you're married to it, for better or for worse—whatever you've **said**, and whatever you've left **unsaid**, you're going to have to live with. And if you insist on sticking with gobbledygook "formula" writing just because everybody's always written that way, you'd better be willing to accept the fact that your "marriage" will usually be **for worse**.

If I were you, I wouldn't want to keep turning out reports that please defense lawyers; I'd want to write things that the **defendant** would have trouble living with. How do you do that? Simple. You write reports that marry the **criminal** to the things **he** did and said. Make it tough on **him** to explain away his conduct. Let **him** do the squirming in front of judge and jury six months later when his words and actions come back to haunt him.

And I'd make it easy on myself. I'd write a report I would have no trouble living with six months or six years later. I'd say things this way:

> *On February 6, 1978, Homicide Detective JOINER told me a woman named J.L. BELT lived in the duplex at 939 East 17th Street.*

Not only is this sentence about 25% shorter than the other one ("Work smarter, not harder"), it's about 250% **more factual**. You could live with it long after it's written, without the uncomfortable cross-examination you saw with the gobbledygook version.

If that advantage sounds good to you, and if you're concerned about whether the criminals you arrest get boxed in or cut loose by your reports, here are my suggestions on how to make it easier on yourself, and rougher on the criminal, to live with your reports.

1. KNOW WHEN AND HOW TO USE QUOTATIONS IN YOUR REPORTS.

Quotation marks around the words you're attributing to someone (witness or arrestee) show that you aren't **interpreting** for the reader—you're letting the reader hear it for himself so he can interpret it anyway he wants to. Correctly using quotations can make your report less conclusionary and more factual. That always makes it easier for you to live with.

For example, how many different ways can someone be obscene? Profane? Abusive? Threatening? Obnoxious? Evasive? Deceptive? These words are NEVER FACTUAL; they're ALWAYS CONCLUSIONARY, because "obscenity" and "profanity" are in the ear of the beholder. You should ALWAYS prefer a factual quotation if the only alternative is a conclusionary interpretation. In each pair of these examples, pretend you wrote the report several months ago, and now you're trying to answer specific questions in court. Ask yourself which version is easier for you to live with, and harder for the crook.

EXAMPLES

CONCLUSIONARY: *I detained him further because when I asked him where he got the TV, his answer was suspicious and unresponsive.*

FACTUAL: *I detained him further because when I asked him where he got the TV, he said: "Hey, man, you ain't got nothing on me . . . you can't prove it's stolen or you wouldn't be hasslin' me.''*

□   □   □

CONCLUSIONARY: *The suspect's language was quite abusive and obnoxious to this officer.*

FACTUAL: *GARRET said: ''You're just a pig! Pigs eat slop. You're a slop-eatin' pig, you know that, Pig?''*

□   □   □

CONCLUSIONARY: *GLASSER was extremely evasive when questioned as to his explanation for being there.*

FACTUAL: *When I asked GLASSER what he was doing there, he said: ''I got my reasons. . . it's a free country, ain't it?''*

□   □   □

Usually, you're going to be doing the crook a favor when you fail to quote some damaging comment he's made, because you're not going to force him to live with it through plea bargaining and trial. (The same goes for witnesses who seem friendly to the arrestee.)

It's fairly common for cops arresting drunk drivers to throw in an editorial line like *"He was un-cooperative and yelled numerous profanities during the arrest."* That's awfully generous of you. It doesn't carry much weight for filing complaints or plea bargaining, and if the defense attorney asks for specifics at trial, you're either going to be guessing or repeating "I don't know" over and over, like a naughty schoolboy. You're having pains living with your report, and the defendant is having fun.

☐ ☐ ☐

Several months ago, I was handling a drunk driving case at the plea bargaining stage, and when I looked at the Highway Patrol Officer's report, it was my turn to grin and the defense lawyer's turn to look uncomfortable. Instead of a lot of generous conclusionary words like "profanities" and "obscenities," the officer had given me (and himself) a lot of verbatim quotes that no defendant could ever live with in front of a respectable jury.

To the question: *"Where are you going?"* the defendant had answered: *"None of your fucking business!"*

To the question: *"How much have you had to drink?"* he said: *"Two fucking cases of beer."*

"Do you know what time it is?"
"Time for you to go fuck yourself!"

"What have you had to eat?"
"I ate your fucking dog-cunt mother."

And on and on it went. Now it was **my** turn to say to the defense lawyer, "Have you read the police report? Do you really want to take this case to trial?" Not only did the defendant plead to the drunk driving charge, he also plead to a charge of disturbing the peace, which I added because of the defendant's language. Without the quotes the officer had married the defendant to, I'd have been lucky to get a drunk driving conviction without a three-day trial. The defendant could have lived with conclusionary words like "profanities" and "obscenities," but he couldn't live with his own words.

☐   ☐   ☐

Another time to prefer quotes to conclusions is when you're writing about words used by a suspect which amount to a refusal, denial, consent, waiver, admission or confession. Otherwise, not only would it be hard for you to live with the questions about what exact words the defendant used that led you to conclude he was refusing, etc., it would be easier for him to offer a different recollection about things he said which did **not** amount to a refusal, etc.

When you write *"BLOCK refused to take a chemical test,"* all you're telling the reader is that Block did or said something that **you** interpreted as a refusal. You're not painting a picture of what you **heard** and saw. And at trial, your conclusions are usually not admissible, so where does that leave us? It leaves us without valuable facts that we need to prove guilt.

Here's an illustration. I once got into a drunk driving trial where, according to the arresting officer, the defendant had "repeatedly refused" to take a chemical test. The defendant was named Sanchez, and at trial he insisted, through a court interpreter, that he neither spoke nor understood any English. His defense that he couldn't possibly refuse an English-language request when he couldn't even understand it sold well with the jury, especially after the officer had to admit that he didn't recall exactly **how** or in what specific words the defendant had "refused" a test. The cop couldn't live with his conclusionary report. Neither could I. The defendant lived with it very comfortably, and he owed his acquittal directly to the same officer who had arrested him. Ironic?

We would have been much better off if the cop had never used the conclusionary word "refused," but had instead married the defendant to his own words! The report could have helped the **prosecution**, instead of the defense, if it had been written like this:

EXAMPLE

> *After I explained the need to take a chemical test, SANCHEZ said, in Spanish-accented English, "Screw you, cop . . . I ain't taking no test, man. Why don't you take it yourself?" I told him he had to take a test or his license would be suspended. He said, "I don't need no license to drive, man. . . I know lots of people drive without a license. You ain't scared me, man, and I ain't taking no stupid test . . . I'll beat this thing, too."*

See the difference? Not a single conclusion or interpretation. The reader gets to "hear" the same things the writer heard. The officer could have lived with something like that—the defendant couldn't.

The same thing goes for these conclusionary interpretations:

EXAMPLES

> • He *denied any involvement in the crime.*

> • *She consented to a search of the trunk.*

> • *Both waived their rights per "Miranda."*

> • *He admitted breaking into the car.*

> • *He confessed to four more burglaries.*

We can't live with junky writing like that; only crooks can. It isn't enough to say that someone "denied" something—you've got to report **how** he "denied" it. Sometimes a spontaneous denial at the time of arrest can be very helpful in convicting someone, because it ties him to a hastily-contrived story that we can knock apart at trial. If you do the criminal the favor of just saying "He denied it," he can then take his own sweet time between booking and trial (maybe six or eight months) to come up with a deliberately-thought-out defense that we may not be able to shake. Don't do the crook the favor of writing a conclusionary report for him to use against us—tie him down to his improbable explanation and make him live with it!

Defendants have a habit of coming back against righteous consents, waivers and admissions. Don't let them. Report their own words, and they're married! Even if they later deny saying the things you've quoted, their testimony can be impeached with their earlier inconsistent statements; that can't be done if all we have in your report are **your** conclusions and interpretations.

☐ ☐ ☐

Another time to prefer quotations is when you're describing something a witness **did** by talking. For instance, instead of saying that someone "indicated" something, tell the reader what **you heard and saw**.

EXAMPLE

CONCLUSIONARY: *Several bloodied men were standing in a group. HUNT indicated that GOULD was the one who had hit him.*

FACTUAL: *I saw about five or six bloodied men standing in a group. HUNT walked up to GOULD, pointed his finger at GOULD and said: "This is the guy that slugged me."*

☐   ☐   ☐

It's possible to "indicate" by talking, by pointing, by drawing pictures, by using sign language, or by nodding your head. When I see an officer put the word "indicated" in a report, it's a tip-off that the officer is giving me his own interpretation of the facts, rather than the straightforward facts. You're not painting a picture when you write that someone "indicated" something; the reader is interested in **how** something was "indicated" to you.

We can't live with the word "indicated," so DON'T USE IT. Instead, tell what you heard and what you saw.

Likewise with "identified." (Some cops like to say "positively identified;" I don't know what the difference is.)

EXAMPLE

CONCLUSIONARY: *She identified the*
suspect PENDER.

FACTUAL: *She said: "That's him.*
Number 3 from the left
. . . no doubt about it,
that's him."
Number 3 from the left
was PENDER.

If it's necessary for you to talk about it further, once you've described the identification, it's alright to use "identified," because both you and the witness now have something you can live with.

□   □   □

Quotations should also be used if the language you use to summarize someone's statement is going to look and sound absurd. No one but cops talk the way cops do. So when you put someone else's plain talk into your official terminology, it usually just makes your witness sound out-of-character.

For instance, one investigator came up with this gobbledygook nonsense when he "interpreted" a statement from a six-year old girl who was the victim of a child molestation:

EXAMPLE

CONCLUSIONARY: *It should be noted that*
on close questioning of

*Maria conducted by
undersigned in-
vestigator, Maria in-
dicated to undersigned
investigator that the
named suspect had
manually fondled her
vaginal area while she
was in a state of undress
brought about by the
named suspect. Further,
according to the victim
Maria, the suspect had
in fact perpetrated
digital insertion into her
vaginal orifice after
briefly massaging her ex-
ternal genitalia with his
hand. It should further
be noted, however, that
Maria seemed unable to
verbalize any particular
distinction between the
telling of a truth and an
untruth, when queried
by undersigned in-
vestigator.*

(Can you imagine some little six-year old girl saying
something like: "And then he perpetrated digital insertion into my vaginal orifice?")

FACTUAL: I questioned Maria and she gave me these answers:

Q: *What did Mr. NORBERT do?*
A: *He rubbed me.*

Q: *What did he rub you with?*
A: *His fingers.*

Q: *Where did he rub you, Maria?*
A: *My pee-pee. There. (She pointed to her pubic area.)*

Q: *Were you wearing your clothes?*
A: *He pulled my panties down, too.*

Q: *Did he stick his finger in your pee-pee?*
A: *Like that (moving her finger back and forth).*

Q: *Now, Maria, do you know what a lie is?*
A: *Yeah. I'm not lying, though.*

Q: *I know you're a good girl. What is a lie?*
A: *(She shrugged her shoulders.)*

Q: *If I said I was a pony, is that a lie?*
A: *I want to go home. (Started crying ... returned to her mother.)*

Both of these versions are about the same length. But this second one, using Maria's own words, is far more believable than the conclusionary gobbledygook, and it gives us a report we can live with.

If the officer who wrote the conclusionary version had to explain to the defense attorney at trial exactly **how** Maria indicated the manual fondling, he'd have to have a pretty good memory. But if he'd written it the **factual** way, with the same amount of work, he could live with the report long after his memory had faded. And we both know that's often the case by the time the case goes to trial.

So. Don't make it look as if little kids talk like cops, or biology teachers, or doctors. They don't. Neither do most of your adult witnesses. Don't create unnecessary work and unnecessary headaches for yourself by translating witnesses' statements from everyday English into gobbledygook, only to face the task of trying to recall the plain English again for the trial jury. That's like doing your interviews in English, then writing all your reports in Japanese, then having to translate back into English when you testify. Only worse. Why go through it? I suggest you **start** in plain English, **stay** in plain English, and you can easily **finish** in plain English.

☐　　　☐　　　☐

In cases where the spoken words themselves are the crime, or any part of it, it is absolutely essential to quote the criminal, rather than rephrasing everything into gobbledygook. This goes for crimes like obscene phone calls, threatening phone calls, conspiracy, bribery, soliciting another crime, sale of stolen property, dope sales, illegal challenges and offers, and making false reports.

I recently saw a vice cop's report on a massage-parlour arrest for soliciting an act of prostitution. The best thing he could have done was to report just **who** said **what**, and in **which order**. Instead, he wrote in language that you can bet neither of them used, and the whole report sounded unrealistic and unconvincing. It went like this:

EXAMPLE

CONCLUSIONARY: *After the suspect had indicated a willingness to perform a variety of different services during a massage, I told her that I did not want any type of altercation resulting from a misunderstanding of the total cost of my massage. Further mutual assurances and negotiations resulted in an agreement for the suspect to perform an act of fellatio in exchange for the price of $35. Thereafter, I identified myself as a police officer and placed the suspect under arrest.*

Remember, now, the **solicitation** is the crime. If you

write a report like that one, you aren't giving yourself any help, because you know darn well you're going to be asked some very specific questions about who said what, and that kind of reporting isn't going to help you remember enough to give the right answers. This is much better:

FACTUAL: *After she told me there were "a lot of little tricks to a good massage, and I'm into all of 'em," we had this exchange.*

ME: *I just want to make sure it's all up front—no arguments later.*

HER: *Yeah, that's cool. You sure you're not a cop?*

ME: *Do I look like a cop? Are you sure you're not a cop? I mean, you could be settin' me up.*

HER: *Don't worry honey. What's it going to be?*

ME: *How about a little head?*

HER: *I get $35, up front, and you give me a one-minute warning. OK?*

ME: *I'm a police officer. You're under arrest.*

☐   ☐   ☐

Here's a couple more:

CONCLUSIONARY: *According to the victim, the caller made several*

| | *obscene comments.* |
| **FACTUAL:** | *FAIRCHILD told me the caller said: "Hey, lady, you got a real sexy voice . . . it gives me a hard-on just thinking about how sweet your pussy must taste."* |

☐   ☐   ☐

CONCLUSIONARY:	*The complainant RICHTER advised me that the caller made numerous threats to RICHTER and members of his family.*
FACTUAL:	*RICHTER told me the caller said: "I'll get you both! I'm gonna blow your brother's head off if I catch him, and I'll burn your place down if I have to, but I'll get even with you!"*

☐   ☐   ☐

I've come across a few cops who have told me they're reluctant to use quotations because they can't always write down everyone's exact words and they don't want to misquote anyone. That's understandable. But it's not insurmountable. You can put quote marks around **exact quotations,** and you can also legitimately use them for **approximate quotations.** All you have to do is make it clear in your report which way you're using them.

If you don't say anything to the contrary, readers will assume quotation marks show **exact** quotes. When you're quoting from memory and you're not prepared to say the quotation is exact, simply say that the conversation is **paraphrased,** or was **substantially** as reported. If you're challenged about it on the stand, you can explain that you wrote it down within 20 minutes (etc.) and that it's either verbatim or very close, and that any difference between what was said and what you wrote, if any, could only be as to words that don't change the meaning (like ''the'' and ''an''). And you might add that you come much closer to a precise quotation 20 minutes after you've heard something than you do 4 months (etc.) later.

The extra mileage we get from even **approximate** quotations offsets any mileage the defense attorney is going to get from showing you can't guarantee 100% accuracy of a quotation. (And if your prosecutor's on the ball, he won't leave that clarification for the defense but will bring it out himself whenever your report shows that you're only claiming to quote **substantially** as you heard it.)

One word of caution about quotations (actually, it applies to everything else you put in a report, too): before you go into the courtroom, be sure that you and any prosecution witness you've quoted have a chance to review the report, under the prosecutor's guidelines, so that you don't go into court testifying from a stale memory and start contradicting your own report. Any police officer who doesn't bother refreshing his recollection about an old arrest from his report before getting on the witness stand is probably going to do more good for the defense than for the prosecution. Check with your local prosecutor about his policy on this.

Okay. When should you prefer a quotation to an interpretation or summary of someone else's statements? Whenever (1) the only other way to report is to use conclusionary words like "suspicious," "profane" and "obnoxious;" (2) the criminal's language is so incriminating, embarrassing or otherwise damaging that its impact is lost without a quote; (3) the suspect or witness says something that amounts to a refusal, denial, consent, waiver, admission or confession; (4) a person said something that you took as an **indication** or **identification;** (5) your version would make it look like someone is talking absurdly out of character (as in the child molest example); and (6) the words themselves constitute the crime, or any element of it.

It's possible I've overlooked some situation where quotations are preferable. Don't worry about it if you come across something else—just remember that the point is to give yourself a report you can live with down the road, and to marry the arrestee and his witnesses to statements they **can't** live with. If that objective calls for a quotation someplace else than the places I've suggested, use it.

2. DON'T ALLOW LEGAL TERMINOLOGY OR VAGUE WORDS TO TAKE THE PLACE OF FACTS.

I once had a cop send over an arrest report to me for a complaint charging assault on an officer and interfering with an officer. As an ex-cop myself, that's the last kind of complaint I want to refuse, especially when someone's locked up in jail and his attorney's already yelling about false-arrest lawsuits. But in two full pages of narrative about the arrest, the only thing the officer had said about what the arrestee had done was this: "This officer was set upon and accosted by subject VALDEZ."

What kind of picture does that paint in your mind? What exactly did Valdez do? You can't tell, can you? Neither could I; on the basis of that report, I didn't have sufficient facts alleged to justify a complaint. "Set upon and accosted" is just a meaningless phrase the cop threw in to avoid putting down the **facts** of what Valdez did.

I couldn't "see" or "hear" anything that went on by reading about how someone was "set upon and accosted." And even if I had issued a complaint, how could a cop live with a report so devoid of facts? Unless he could remember precisely what Valdez did when the trial came up months later, he **couldn't** live with it. And even if he started testifying to some specifics, he'd be back to the questions about why he didn't put these significant details in his report.

Another common one is "a struggle ensued." In our business, it's pretty important to know **how** a struggle ensued. Who started it? What did he do? What happened next? How long did it last? How did it end? Was anyone hurt? Where? How? When you go out to the scene and get the answers to those questions, don't shortchange your readers (including yourself when it's time to testify) by lazily declaring that "a struggle ensued," and leaving out the facts.

The same comments apply to words like "assault," "attack," "confront," "molest," "annoy," "rape," "intimidate," "force," "coerce," "threaten," "persuade," "induce," and so on. Don't use such words unless you've **first** painted a factual picture of what was said and done to constitute the "assault," etc.

3. DON'T MAKE UNSUPPORTED ASSERTIONS ABOUT SOMEONE ELSE'S ABILITIES, PERCEPTIONS, OR STATE OF MIND.

When you write that someone "could" or "could not" do something, you're drawing a conclusion.

Why not simply say that he "did" or "did not" do it, and let the reader draw his own conclusions?

EXAMPLES

CONCLUSIONARY: *When instructed to do so, he could not touch the tip of his nose with his fingertips.*

FACTUAL: *When I told him to touch the tip of his nose with his fingertips, he touched the bridge of his nose.*

☐   ☐   ☐

CONCLUSIONARY: *She was unable to walk a straight line.*

FACTUAL: *She did not walk in a straight line.*

☐   ☐   ☐

The only way you can tell that someone else is seeing or hearing something is if he says so, or he seems to be reacting to some sight or sound. Say which it is.

EXAMPLES

CONCLUSIONARY: *He was bent forward. When he straightened up and saw me, he turned and walked away.*

FACTUAL: *He was bent forward. When he straightened up, he was facing me. Our eyes met, then he turned and walked away.*

☐   ☐   ☐

CONCLUSIONARY: *He heard the crash and took off running.*

FACTUAL: *At the moment of the crash, he jerked his head around toward the collision, then took off running.*

☐   ☐   ☐

CONCLUSIONARY: *They both saw what happened.*

FACTUAL: *Both said they saw what happened.*

☐   ☐   ☐

Don't write like a mindreader unless you can qualify in court. Show the **source** of your conclusions.

For instance, the reason you can tell someone is happy, unhappy, angry, excited, nervous, upset, relieved, scared, or any of those other things that go on primarily in his mind, is because he **told** you so, or you **saw** and **heard** things from which you can draw reasonable conclusions. If someone else's mental state

is important to report, give yourself some facts to support your conclusions, so you're not left at time of
trial without anything to testify to (you can't generally testify to "conclusions" and "speculation").

That also applies to statements about someone else
"trying" or "attempting" to do something. A person who's jiggling a wire coat hanger through the
windwing of a car may be trying to steal the car, or he
may be the owner, trying to get back into his car after
locking himself out, or he may be trying to remove a
hanger that someone else left there, or he may be
making a movie on auto theft with a hidden cam-
era, etc.

When you roll up and see what he's doing, you
may draw some conclusion about what he's **trying** to
do—your **observation** is a **fact**: you saw him jiggling a
coat hanger through the windwing; your **conclusion** is
a guess or a deduction: it may prove to be right or
wrong, when you get more facts, but your conclusion
is not a fact, at least in the legal business, until some
judge or jury hears all your other facts and decides
that your conclusion was right. So instead of reporting
"I saw him trying to steal the car," you're better off
saying "I saw him jiggling a wire coat hanger through
the windwing on the driver's side."

As you write, just remember that someday, when
you've got to live with your report, you're going to be
asked: "What exactly was he doing that led you to
believe, Officer, that he was 'trying' to do what

you've said?'' Instead of a conclusionary word like ''trying,'' prefer factual ones that show the **source** of your conclusion (''I saw . . .,'' ''I heard . . .,'' ''he said . . .,'' etc.).

4. WHEN NECESSARY, SHOW THE FACTS BEHIND YOUR STATE OF MIND.

A few pages back, I suggested that ''profanity'' is in the ear of the beholder. Well, ''suspicious'' is in the **mind** of the beholder. So are ''furtive,'' ''strange,'' ''belligerent,'' ''uncooperative,'' ''abnormal,'' ''typical,'' and other such words. They're conclusions, every one. You've got to support them with facts which show their sources.

Your own state of mind is generally important only when you have to explain or justify something you did. As you know, you've got to give details (and I mean **details**—not just an outline) of your knowledge, experience, observations, **and the conclusions you drew from them** when you're reporting about probable cause for a stop/detention/arrest, or a search or seizure, or a warrantless entry into a home. It is inexcusably inadequate for you to simply say: ''He made a furtive movement,'' instead of telling what you saw him do, and why you considered that to be ''furtive'' (as a matter of fact, I wouldn't even use ''furtive''—I think it's an unfamiliar word to too many people in your reading audience).

Likewise with these unacceptable phrases:

EXAMPLES

"She was acting suspicious."

"Their conduct was strange."

"She was unusual in appearance."

"He seemed to be uncooperative."

"The suspect was becoming belligerent."

"His attitude had become combative in nature."

"I realized this was out of the ordinary."

"They did not act like typical motorists."

"He fit the suspect's description."

"I felt they might possibly be armed."

"It was obvious he was under the influence."

"Exigent circumstances existed."

Standing alone, without any supporting facts (which is how I often see them), these conclusionary statements are not enough to explain or justify anything. You've got to include what the judges, in their own brand of gobbledygook, call "articulable facts." (That just means facts you can tell about.) To be sure you and I can live with your report, tell **how** she was suspicious; **what** was unusual; **why** you thought they might be armed, and so forth. Justify your state of mind with **facts**.

5. DON'T WRITE A "WHODUNIT."

Since I devoted a chapter to the "whodunit" problem, we don't need to go over it here, except to point out that "whodunits" are impossible for you to live with.

EXAMPLES

WHODUNIT: *Witnesses at the scene advised that KENNER was the driver of the truck.*

(Which witnesses said so? How did they know he was the driver?)

FACTUAL: *CLEARY and TAYLOR both told me they saw KENNER driving the truck.*

□   □   □

WHODUNIT: *Lt. Thomas reinterviewed all three suspects and was informed that the gun was in the toilet tank.*

(Which one of the three suspects said this?)

FACTUAL: *Lt. Thomas reinterviewed all three suspects. OROSCO told him the gun was in the toilet tank.*

□   □   □

WHODUNIT: *While talking to Mr. and Mrs. DILLON, I learned that the van had been seen*

> *parked on the street the day*
> *before the burglary.*

(Who told you? Who saw the van?)

FACTUAL: *While I was talking to Mr.*
             and Mrs. DILLON, Mrs.
             DILLON told me that she
             saw the van parked on the
             street the day before the
             burglary.

□   □   □

Once again, to appreciate the difference, imagine yourself trying to testify to details at a trial several months after you've written the report, and ask yourself which of the preceding versions in each example is easier to live with. (Or, put yourself in my place when it's time to subpena the right witnesses to make the driver, or approach one of the three suspects with an offer for his testimony, or call the proper witness to the stand to talk about the van. With the "whodunit" versions, you can't figure out who your witnesses are, can you? Neither can I.)

6. RECAP

To make it easier for you to review from time to time without having to re-read, I'll put the troublesome words in a chart, with suggested alternatives. Before we get there, however, I promised to give you a better approach to the defense attorney's

typical questions about things that aren't in your
report. Here's how I would answer:

Q: *Now, Officer, you wrote a report about
this arrest, didn't you?*

A: *Yes, sir.*

Q: *And wasn't the purpose of that report to
record all the important information
about this case?*

A: *Not exactly. It's hardly ever possible to
record all the information, so my report is
usually more like a **summary** than a complete account of every single thing.*

Q: *But you do try to include in your report
all the important details, don't you?*

A: *If I can tell at the time which details are
going to prove to be important, yes sir. I
can't always foresee what will turn out to
be important in every case.*

Q: *I take it, Officer, that these events were
clearer in your mind when you wrote the
report than they are now, some six
months later, right?*

A: *Some of them were, naturally, but some
things are just as clear in my mind now as
they ever were.*

Q: *Did you deliberately leave out any significant details when you wrote the report?*

A: *Not deliberately, but necessarily. Since I*

can't possibly put down everything, or anticipate what others will consider to be "significant," I do my best to give an accurate summary of what happened.

Q: *Don't you think it's significant to know which one of these men hit the other one first?*

A: *Yes.*

Q: *And it's your testimony today that you saw Sharp hit Peters first, is that right?*

A: *That's right.*

Q: *Now Officer, did you put that in your report?*

A: *No, I didn't.*

Q: *Would you care to explain to the jury, Officer, whether you left that out of your report because you didn't consider it significant at the time, or whether it's something you've just now recalled, six months later?*

A: *I'd be glad to explain it. I've been on the witness stand testifying about this for an hour and twenty minutes. I wrote my report in fifteen minutes. If I could afford to spend as much time writing each report as I spend testifying, I suppose I could include as many details, but I can't do that, or I wouldn't get any police work done. So I try to make every report a fair and ac-*

> *curate summary, and in doing that, I*
> *realize there are going to be times when*
> *something will be left out that may turn*
> *out later to be significant. Usually, if it's*
> *that significant, it will stand out in my*
> *memory, the way it does now that I saw*
> *Sharp hit Peters first.*

These are more truthful answers to the questions. But far better than knowing how to handle such questions is knowing how to **avoid** them: write a report you can live with—leave out all the gobbledygook, all the labels, all the whodunits and all the unsupported conclusions . . . marry the defendant and his witnesses to every material word and phrase they utter, and you're hardly ever going to have to answer embarrassing and damaging questions about what is and what isn't in your report. Make it easier on yourself—work smarter, not harder.

You can't live with these . . .	. . . so use these, instead
indicated refused admitted confessed denied consented identified waived profanity threatening obscene evasive unresponsive deceptive	a verbatim or approximate quotation of what was said
assaulted attacked accosted confrontation escalated struggle ensued resisted battered intimidated bullied forced	a factual account of who did what

You can't live with these . . .	. . . so use these, instead
angry upset nervous excited happy unhappy intentional accidental attempted heard saw knew thought	when you're attributing these to someone else, the **source** of your conclusions
matching the description suspicious furtive strange abnormal typical uncooperative belligerent combative obnoxious abusive exigent	the reasons for your belief that these apply

CLEANING UP

I have a few final suggestions on how to unclutter your reports. One is to leave out the "introductory" statement of your narrative if it's only a repetition of facts already contained in the blanks of the standard report heading. Most report forms have you fill in a blank for the date, time, location, and people and their roles, before you ever get to the place where your narrative begins.

Despite this, many officers think they have to have some kind of "lead in" statement in which they do something like this:

EXAMPLE

ARTIFICIAL: *On above date and time, undersigned officer responded to above location*

> *reference above-described*
> *call, contacting above-listed*
> *witness/informant, who pro-*
> *vided the following informa-*
> *tion.*
> *Witness/Informant*
> *TALMADGE related that*
> *when he arrived at his place*
> *of residence . . .*

Why repeat facts that have already been given? What does that first sentence in the example (and your own reports) add? Just work and bulk. They say that bulk in your diet makes your food easier to digest, but as a principal reader and user of your reports, I can assure you that bulk in your writing makes your reports **harder** to digest.

If you leave out all the non-factual bulk, it will be easier for you to concentrate on being sure you include all the factual information your report is supposed to contain. I've found that writers who clutter their reports with a lot of ''stock'' police phrases often become so preoccupied with wordy expressions that they leave out the important things—like the elements of the crime and the evidence against the arrestee.

Don't concentrate your efforts on copying the ''professional'' police writing **style**; it's the **content** that counts. Instead of taking up time and space with a needless repetition, get right to the facts:

NATURAL: *At the scene, TALMADGE told me that when he came home . . .*

☐   ☐   ☐

When you have to report a lengthy statement you took from a suspect or a witness, don't start ten or twenty sentences by saying: "And he further related that . . ." Just say it once, and then give his statement.

EXAMPLE

ARTIFICIAL: *This officer conducted an interview with victim CRAIG who related the following information to this officer. CRAIG stated that his car had been broken into. He further related that his CB radio had been stolen. He stated that he parked his car at 11:00 p.m. last night, and according to his statement, he gave no one permission to take the radio. CRAIG further related that he discovered that the radio was missing at 6:15 a.m. this morning. He related that he had not seen or heard anything unusual during the*

> *night, but he did state that his dog had barked around midnight.*

NATURAL:
> *I asked CRAIG what happened and he said this: He parked his car last night at 11:00 and found this morning at 6:15 that it had been broken into. His CB radio was taken, without his permission. His dog barked around midnight, but CRAIG didn't see or hear anything unusual during the night.*

All the same **facts**, but 50% less work. (Incidentally, it's important for you to notice in my examples that work is **never** saved by leaving out **information**—only by eliminating excess words and phrases that contain no information themselves and tend to get the facts buried under a pile of verbiage. Following these suggestions should be like losing weight through exercise: only the fat goes, while the muscles get toned into shape. Losing the fat from your reports will allow you to spend all of your efforts where they belong—communicating information.)

☐   ☐   ☐

Don't use long sentences or paragraphs—they're too hard to read and digest. I've seen sentences that ran on for half a typewritten page. And I've seen paragraphs three pages long.

All the reading we've done in our lives has gotten us into the habit of taking in groups of words before they register. We look for a place to pause and let them sink in. If the end of the sentence is too long in coming, some of the words get lost. The same goes for paragraphs.

Give yourself, and your reader, a place to pause and digest each sentence, and each paragraph. That makes it easier for the reader to take in all the information without having to re-read.

☐   ☐   ☐

Try not to jump around. Report things in the same order as they happened. Otherwise, you may leave out things you should have put in. Also, it's easier for the reader to follow your report if you don't keep jumping around and going back and forth.

EXAMPLE

ARTIFICIAL: *At 11:35 p.m. Officer GAINES detained a suspect, later identified as subject JOHNSON, following a carstop of a truck at 1st and Elm.*

The suspect had worn a mask throughout the incident, and

*a red ski mask was later
found in the bed of
JOHNSON'S truck. It should
be noted that when I had
earlier interviewed the victim
MILLER, he had in fact
described the mask as a red
ski mask.*

*It was later determined that
the truck JOHNSON was
driving had a broken right
rear taillight. MILLER had
previously reported that the
suspect left driving a truck
with a broken right rear
taillight.*

*It should be noted that the
red ski mask was in fact
located by Officer GAINES.*

NATURAL: *MILLER said the suspect wore
a red ski mask and fled in a
truck that had a broken right
taillight.*

*Officer GAINES stopped
such a truck at 11:35 p.m. at
1st and Elm, and detained
the driver, JOHNSON. Of-
ficer GAINES found a red ski
mask in the truck bed.*

Both examples contain identical facts, but putting

them in proper order saves a lot of wasteful repetition (60% less work). More importantly, the natural version is far easier to read and follow. (By the way, you don't need the word "rear" to describe taillights—there aren't any other kind.)

☐   ☐   ☐

You don't really have time to write, and I don't have time to read, extra words that add no meaning. So don't put in any fillers. The worst one is probably "It should be noted that . . ."

What do these words add to the meaning? Nothing. What factual information do they contain? None. **Everything** you write in your report is going to be "noted." It isn't as if those of us who use your reports skim over them, looking for the magic words, "It should be noted that," and reading only those sentences with that preface.

When you toss "It should be noted that" around in front of every other sentence, all you're doing is padding your reports with a five-word phrase that adds extra work for you, the typist, and the reader. It adds no extra information—just extra work.

My own unofficial survey of reports peppered with "It should be noted that" shows that it pops up an average of ten times per report. That means that an officer who writes six reports per day is adding about 72,000 words of pure padding per year. Multiply that by the number of officers in your department, and you can figure out how much effort your department wasted last year on just that one useless phrase. Mind boggling?

And look how easy it is to simply throw it out:

EXAMPLES

ARTIFICIAL: *It should be noted that JAMES fainted.*

NATURAL: *JAMES fainted.*

□   □   □

ARTIFICIAL: *It should be noted that the pistol was loaded.*

NATURAL: *The pistol was loaded.*

□   □   □

ARTIFICIAL: *It should be noted that I ducked.*

NATURAL: *I ducked.*

In case you need a reminder: "Work smarter, not harder."

□   □   □

A lot of us are unquestioning copycats—we see something done one way over and over, so **we** do it the same way, and never bother wondering why. How many times have you seen this kind of thing:

> *We found two (2) briefcases, each containing five (5) handguns, for a total of ten (10) handguns.*

Did you ever wonder why people write out the

number and then put the numeral beside it in parentheses? I wonder, too. As a lawyer, I don't know any reason for it. I **do** know a good reason **not** to do it: it's unnecessary work for the writer and the reader.

Likewise, when the arithmetic is as simple as 2 x 5, you don't need to do it for the reader. Just say:

We found two briefcases, each containing five handguns.

☐ ☐ ☐

People who read your reports realize that unless you say you recognized someone from a prior experience, the people you write about start out as unidentified strangers, and sometime during your dealings with them you find out their names. So this isn't necessary:

The driver, later identified as BURNS, raised his hands.

The "later identified as" can be reasonably inferred, and though it's only three extra words, a report which mentions eight or ten people who get "later identified as" can get cluttered. Everyone knows you didn't write your report until **after** you'd found out who you were dealing with, so just say,

BURNS, the driver, raised his hands.

☐ ☐ ☐

There's a place for the qualifier "described as." The place is before descriptions you got from a victim or witness and haven't verified with your own eyes and ears. For example, when you put out a broadcast for a hit-and-run vehicle, and you're relying on a witness's description, there's nothing wrong with this:

> *The suspect vehicle is described as a white over blue 1974 Thunderbird with recent front-end damage.*

You didn't see the car yourself. It may turn out to have been a white over gray 1976 Ford Elite. It's okay to qualify your description by saying, in effect, that this is how someone else described it to you.

On the other hand, when you see someone or something with your own two eyes, **don't** say that he, or it, is "described as." For example, if you had seen the hit-run accident occur, you would just broadcast what you saw. And in writing the accident report, don't say,

> *Elm street is described as a two-lane blacktop street.*

You make it sound like you never saw the street personally, you're just taking someone's word for it. Say,

> *Elm Street is a two-lane blacktop.*

Some cops think that "described as" are magical police words that absolutely must go in front of every single description. No so. Use them only to qualify an unverified description—not to clutter up a statement about a person or a thing that you yourself saw.

I can tell from reading reports that a lot of police officers think the longer they make a report by throwing in every excess word and phrase they can think of, the more complete it will be, and the more thorough they will appear. Again, of course, it's not so. They just make it harder to pick out the information among the verbiage.

Other cops think there's a "standard" length for a given kind of crime report, and they try to stretch or squeeze so that every drunk driver report is exactly three pages, every auto burglary is two, and every gang fight is six. Wrong again. The length of every report should depend on one thing: how much information you have to report.

And though you can't possibly put in every single step you take, every observation you make, and every word your witnesses utter, you have to include every relevant fact you can to paint a complete picture for your reader, without whodunits, and in language you and I can live with down the road.

The best report is one that's natural, straightforward, accurate and complete, with no fillers or clutter. That's the kind that's easiest to write, easiest to read, and easiest for us to live with. It can help justice get done, instead of helping justice get smothered under an avalanche of vague, obscure, ambiguous and meaningless words and phrases.

If you've been guilty of turning out gobbledygook reports, I suggest you start now to clean them up. Make it easy on yourself (and me, too).

□

SAMPLE
REPORT
THE WAY WE'VE ALWAYS DONE IT

To show you how all the different writing problems can combine to make an unreadable report, here is an abbreviated edition of a lengthy report that crossed my desk a few weeks ago. As you wade through it, ask yourself whether you think the officer is writing naturally or artificially, and whether he wrote this report in order to communicate, or just to impress.

This report is followed by my own version of the same information, and to make a comparison easier, I've numbered the paragraphs of both reports.

The standard heading of the report told me it concerned a residential burglary arrest, on a certain date, at a certain time, and at a certain place. Two arrested persons were named and fully described. The victim and one witness were listed, and the recovered property fully described. What follows is about one-fifth of the original narrative.

1. *On the above date and time, Reporting Officer responded to the referenced location in regards to an area check. It should be noted that upon pulling adjacent to the south boundary fence of Lincoln Elementary School, which is situated at the above-described location, Reporting Officer observed two male subjects, later identified as Suspects No. 1 and 2, to be emerging from the heavy dense fog which had blanketed much of the city on this particular night and time. Due to the heavy fog the two figures actually appeared somewhat distorted in appearance and as they continued to proceed in the direction of the above-mentioned pedestrian exit gate, Reporting Officer proceeded to stop Reporting Officer's patrol vehicle and thereupon illuminated the immediate area of the pedestrian exit gate with a searchlight in an effort to more clearly perceive both subjects and ascertain their particular activity. As the*

subjects approached the pedestrian exit gate it was then noted by Reporting Officer that both subjects at that time appeared to be carrying component parts to a stereo set. It was further noted that the subject that was following the first was wearing black gloves which appeared very odd at this hour of the night, being that the weather did not depict severe enough elements that would in fact warrant the use of gloves.

2. *Upon the subjects becoming cognizant of the presence of Reporting Officer's patrol vehicle and the illumination emitting from same, the two parties discarded the property in their possession and immediately at this time turned and fled back through the pedestrian exit gate through which they had in fact previously approached.*

3. *At this point in time these discarded items were inspected by Reporting Officer. It should be noted that Reporting Officer peered about the immediate area and in doing so utilized the beam from Reporting Officer's flashlight to possibly locate other items of property; however, none were found at this point in time. It was with this effort that Reporting Officer noted that tracks leading from the immediate area of the property were extremely visible, and little or no effort was needed to retrace the* *direction of these particular tracks to the pedestrian exit gate leading from the school premises of Lincoln Elementary School. It should be noted that prior to this Officer exiting the patrol vehicle to further investigate this matter, the dispatcher had been informed by Reporting Officer of the suspicious circumstances involving the fleeing parties from the immediate area of Lincoln Elementary School, as well as the fact that property had in fact been discarded by the subjects prior to taking flight. Shortly thereafter, Officers Blaine and Tichenor responded to the area to assist in the investigation of this matter.*

4. *This Officer proceeded along the west side of the school premises toward a residence, still following the dew soaked tracks, where they disappeared at the fence line separating the front of the residence at 111 W. Broadway from the rear, indicating that the suspects had scaled the fence into the back yard. Reporting Officer also scaled the fence leading to the rear of the residence, following the exact pattern believed to have been taken by the two fleeing subjects. It should be noted that at this time, the footprints were again observed in the immediate area of the fence in the dew soaked grass, still continuing southbound towards the extreme south boundary of the*

residence. At this time Officers Blaine and Tichenor responded to the immediate area of the residence and a search of the shrubbery was conducted. It should be noted that while in the immediate area, this Officer observed a 17' boat which had been parked in the extreme southeast corner of the residence by the owners, with flowers and shrubbery around its immediate sides.

5. *In checking through the shrubbery alongside the aforementioned boat, a male Negro adult subject was detected, lying in a prone position on the paved area of the patio portion of the lawn behind the aforementioned boat. As Reporting Officer placed a firm grasp on his shoulder and clothing, Reporting Officer so instructed the party to remove himself from the pavement. The subject did not comply readily to this request. It should be noted that at this particular time, this Officer had unholstered his service revolver and again repeated the request, nudging at the party in order to make him cognizant of the fact that Reporting Officer was in fact armed and that any abrupt and uncertain movements would possibly prove unfavorable to his state of being. The subject began to verbally vacillate with this Officer, denying any complicity in any criminal ac-*

tivity and indicating a curiosity as to the exact state of affairs as to why he was being pursued. It was necessary to forcibly remove the subject from the ground, being that there was no doubt at this particular time in this Officer's mind that this was in fact one of the subjects I had observed and followed, and that the other remaining suspect was no doubt in close proximity. The suspect in custody was then searched, restrained and handcuffed and instructed not to make any attempt to flee from the immediate area, for insurance against which he was then placed back down on his stomach in a prone position.

6. While Reporting Officer had been thus engaged in the location and apprehension of Suspect Number 1, later identified as one LUTHER, Kenneth James, DOB of 7-12-48, Suspect Number 2, later identified as a JORDAN, Willard Dean, DOB of 9-15-50, and described as a male white adult subject, 5-10, 150 lbs, brown hair, brown eyes, and having an AKA of KARCHER, Willard Leon, was apprehended nearby. At this time, both subjects were given a Miranda advisement from a standard card carried for this particular purpose, and each subject in fact elected to waive his Miranda rights. Both subjects emphatically

denied having any knowledge of the circumstances surrounding the items of stereo equipment.

7. It should be noted that both subjects were then left in the rear seat of Officer Blaine's patrol vehicle. It should be noted further that prior to this, Officer Blaine had in fact taken the liberty of activating his unit's cassette recorder which recorded the individual conversations of both suspects. The recording, after being played back upon return of Officers to the vehicle, disclosed that the suspects were discussing the likelihood of the burglary being discovered and the possibility of them being implicated in the matter. All of this recorded information was subsequently played back to one of the suspects in this case, that being Suspect No. 1, who was then willing to give a complete account of what had occurred in relation to the subsequent apprehension by this Officer.

8. Suspect No. 1, after having been reminded of his Miranda rights and in effect waiving same verbally, related that he and Suspect No. 2 had selected a residence at 2312 S. Magnolia to perpetrate a burglary. Suspect No. 1 related that this was done as a result of the residence having only one light emitting from its interior and no car observed in

the driveway of same. Suspect No. 1 went
on to state that Suspect No. 2 at this time
approached the residence and unlocked the
side gate to the rear yard area. Suspect No.
1 informed this Officer that Suspect No. 2
at this time removed the screen and entered
into the bathroom through a previously
partially-opened bathroom window.
Suspect No. 1 accompanied him at this
time. Upon reaching the interior of the
residence, Suspect No. 1 related that the
stereo components were removed. He
related that after obtaining these items,
both subjects then exited by means of the
front door of the residence and proceeded
to traverse the Lincoln Elementary School
yard, emerging from the pedestrian exit
gate and visually confronting this Officer,
then discarding the same property and fleeing on foot.

9. Suspect No. 2 remained adamant in his
denial of any involvement, even when con-
fronted with the tape recording of the conversation, as well as information which had
in fact been revealed to Reporting Officer
by Suspect No. 1, that being subject
LUTHER. Suspect No. 2 stuck to his own
improbable version of the events, exempli-
fying no consciousness of guilt nor
remorsefulness for the incident which had

occurred. It should also be noted that Suspect JORDAN was extremely uncooperative from beginning to end, and at one point in time was actually on the brink of becoming a combatant arrestee with his failure to comply with this Officer's verbal instructions. It should be further noted, in addition, that it was necessary to forcibly impose the Officers' will upon JORDAN in order to proceed with the booking and other formalities necessary to conclude his processing into the county jail.

10. *For the record, it should be pointed out that additional information was obtained via telephonic contact with Victim LINDSAY in regards to the property identification, and it was confirmed that the recovered stereo component parts were in fact those belonging to Victim LINDSAY, reference the identical brand name and serial numbers accounted for by the victim. For additional personnel in regards to supplemental information refer to original report by Officer Blaine.*

The gloves worn by suspect JORDAN, together with the tape recording referred to above, were booked into evidence locker 4.

□

SAMPLE
REPORT
THE WAY IT SHOULD BE DONE

I told you the example you just read was edited from an actual report which was roughly five times as long. But as they say, enough is too much.

To reduce this kind of mess to readable English in a report that doesn't do the criminal any favors, I had to make some assumptions about things you can't tell from the whodunit gobbledygook. Where you see that I've left some things out, it's either because they're repetitions of facts normally contained in the standard heading, or they just don't have any meaning.

1. *While I was patrolling along the south side of Lincoln Elementary School, I saw LUTHER and JORDAN coming toward me in the heavy fog, leaving the school grounds through a pedestrian gate. I stopped my police car, shined the searchlight on the gate, and saw that both men were carrying stereo components. Even though it was only about 70°, JORDAN was wearing black gloves.*

2. *As the spotlight hit them, both men dropped the components and ran back through the gate. I radioed the dispatcher, told him where I was and what I had seen, and asked for a backup officer.*

3. *I got out of my car and looked around with my flashlight for more property; I didn't find any. The grass was wet with dew, and I saw footprints around the components and the gate. Officers BLAINE and TICHENOR pulled up and I showed them what I had found and told them what I had seen.*

4. *I followed the footprints across the west side of the schoolyard to a fence, and climbed over it into the back yard of the house at 111 W. Broadway. I followed the tracks to the southeast corner of the back yard and saw a boat there among some shrubbery. Officers BLAINE and TICHENOR came*

along behind me, and we searched the yard for the two men.

5. Officer BLAINE found LUTHER lying face-down on a patio behind the boat, and said "Don't move." I went over and held onto LUTHER'S shoulder to be sure he was under control, and then I told him to get up. He didn't move. Not knowing whether he was armed, I drew my pistol and said "Police Officer. Get on your feet, slowly."

6. Meanwhile, Officer TICHENOR had found JORDAN behind a doghouse. I got LUTHER up and walked him about thirty feet away, so JORDAN wouldn't overhear. Then I read his rights to him from my "Miranda" card. I asked if he understood; he said: "Yeah." I asked if he would talk to me; he said: "I'll talk to you, man, but I ain't done nothin' illegal. This here's my uncle's house is all."

I said: "Where'd you guys get the stereo stuff?" LUTHER said: "You're crazy . . . I don't know anything about any stereo."

I left LUTHER with Officer BLAINE and went to JORDAN. I read his rights from the card and asked if he understood. He said: "Umm." I said: "Is that a 'yes' or a 'no'?" He said: "Yes." I asked him if he would talk about what he was doing there

162/THE NEW POLICE REPORT MANUAL

*and where he got the stereo. He said: "I
don't know what you're talking about . . .
go pound sand."*

7. *Officer BLAINE brought his car around to
the front of the house and left a tape
recorder on in the front seat. We put
LUTHER and JORDAN in the back seat
and left them alone for a couple of minutes.
DUVALL came out of the house and I asked
him if either of the men was his nephew.
He said they were not.*

*I got the tape recorder, took LUTHER out
of the car, and played the tape to him. On
it, the two of them talked about a burglary
and the stereo components. After he heard
it, LUTHER said: "OK. That's how it happened, like we said there. I knew he was
gonna get me in trouble."*

8. *I said: "Remember the rights I read you,
Kenneth? You still want to give them up
and talk to me?" He said: "Yeah." I
said: "OK. How did this whole thing happen to you, Kenneth?"*

*LUTHER gave substantially the following
account. JORDAN picked out a house at
2312 S. Magnolia to break into. The house
had only one light on inside, and no car in
the driveway. They went through a side gate*

and JORDAN took off the bathroom window screen. They climbed through the already-open window, went into the living room and took the turntable and receiver, and went out through the front door. They cut across the schoolyard, and when they saw my police car, they dropped the stereo and ran.

9. *After talking to LUTHER, I went back to JORDAN and told him what was on the tape and what LUTHER had told me. JORDAN said: "I still don't know what you're trying to pull, but I ain't admittin' nothin', cause I ain't done shit." I arrested both men and drove them to the jail. During booking, JORDAN kept his hands clasped together when I told him to hold them out for fingerprinting. I pulled his hands apart so he could be printed.*

10. *I phoned LINDSAY and asked him to check for his stereo. He came back and told me it was missing. He looked up his information and gave the same brand and serial numbers as the recovered items, which BLAINE brought in.*

    I put the components, the tape recording, and JORDAN'S gloves in evidence locker 4.

    Officer BLAINE wrote a supplemental report.

☐   ☐   ☐

Even though I expanded some incomplete passages and substituted complete quotations in place of single words like "denial," I still spent only about 50% as much time and effort as the "Reporting Officer" did. And what's far more important, the second version is more readable, more factual, and more useful from a prosecution standpoint.

Don't mistake my sample version as a model of **police work**—it's only meant to show you how to **write**, and I was working with information that was already restricted by the original report. Actually, if I had been the cop on the scene, with a talky suspect and a handy tape recorder, you'd better believe Luther's cop-out would have gone onto that tape, too.

And whether I had a tape recorder or had to write notes for what was going into my report, I'd have been a lot more curious and a lot more precise about Luther's activities while I had him talking. At a minimum, I'd either record or jot down these questions and Luther's answers (in quotes—so he couldn't live with my report after the defense attorney told him how dumb he was to cop out, and how he'd be better off if it turned out the cop just made that part up):

— *Whose idea was it to hit a house?*
— *You knew you were going to be committing a burglary when you climbed in*

through the bathroom window, didn't you, Kenneth?

— *Did you already know what kind of stuff you were going to try to steal?*

— *Had you guys talked about what you'd do if someone came in and caught you? I mean, you took in something for self-defense, right? What was Willy carrying, a gun or a knife?*

— *Where did he ditch it?*

— *What did you have? etc.*

— *You guys obviously knew what you're doing—do you think you could estimate how many houses you've taken stuff from? etc.*

— *I know you've got to get rid of the stuff and turn it into cash. Where do you usually sell it? etc.*

— *I guess you guys were going to score some dope with some of the money—what were you going to do with the rest of it?*

— *Have you got a pretty good connection? etc.*

— *Now that you're being honest with me, and it looks like you're tired of being a dummy, what else can you tell me that I'd want to know?*

Even though some of these questions may be

dreaming, depending on how hard and wise Luther turns out to be and what kind of rapport the cop could get going, they're the kinds of things I'd at least be curious enough to try out on someone who's standing around copping out to a night-time residential burglary. If you get lucky, of course, you add a weapons charge, clear paper on some other burglaries, or get a lead on a fence or a dope dealer. You sure don't get lucky if you don't even bother asking.

And at least, if you tie Luther to some incriminating quotations about **this** case, you'll make it hard for him to have a change of heart.

(This isn't a book on how to interrogate, but since I used the burglary example to illustrate **writing** problems, I wanted to caution you that it is **not** an example of the best possible police work.)

□

WHAT WOULD
HAPPEN IF...?

I think there are two things in books that most people never bother reading. One is a foreword; the other is a footnote. So this book doesn't have either.

As I warned you in the first few pages, some of my writing suggestions may be a little hard for some cops—especially oldtimers—to swallow. Luckily, you don't have to be a guinea pig to try them out. I've been preaching plain-talk report writing since 1975. The guinea pigs (no pun intended) have already tried it out, and they seem to be thriving on it.

I've had the chance to talk to hundreds of officers in the course of seminars and lectures for members of several dozen police, highway patrol, and sheriff's agencies. Through the offices of the California Commission on Peace Officer Standards and Training, a booklet which was the forerunner of this book was distributed to each police chief and sheriff in California in 1977. Many of those departments have given me feedback on their successful transition from stilted writing to straight talk; I know of no department that's had any unfavorable results from it.

And I've had similar favorable feedback from report writing instructors at police academies and in police science classrooms. But if the proof is in the pudding, the best feedback of all has been in watching the reports that come into our office for prosecution turn, almost overnight, from hopeless gobbledygook into clearly-written, factual investigative reports that I have no trouble using against crooks.

As it must be for everyone else who invites something new to be tried in place of something that's old and comfortable, I've talked to a few people who simply refuse to try any of these suggestions, insisting that it couldn't possibly be that easy to improve report writing. One lieutenant told me: ''We've been writing reports the same way for eighteen years—we don't need any lawyer telling us how to write a report.''

And one officer asked me during a seminar if I wasn't asking him to write in a ''Dick and Jane'' style. I told him I didn't think he had to go that far to simplify his writing, but given a choice between this:

>*Dick sees Jane*

and this:

>*It should be noted that a male white juvenile subject, identified as subject Dick, in fact visually observes a female white juvenile subject, identified as subject Jane,*

I'll take "Dick sees Jane" anyday.

What would happen if you and your department wrote every report in straightforward, factual plain talk? I've seen what has happened in other departments—most or all of these things:

>*Less police time writing reports.*
>*More police time in the field.*
>*Less typing time.*
>*Less copying time and expense.*
>*Less filing space and expense.*
>*Less reading time by investigators and supervisors.*
>*More time for investigating and supervising*
>*Less reading time by prosecutors.*
>*Less confusion as to what the report says.*
>*Less duplicative work.*
>*More factual reports.*
>*Better police work.*
>*More reports approved.*

Fewer rewrites.
More complaints approved.
More defense motions denied.
Fewer defense motions filed.
Higher sentences on negotiated pleas.
Better police testimony.
Worse defendant testimony.
More convictions.
Fewer trials.
More pleas.
Less court time for officers.

Heard enough? Wouldn't even two or three of those results justify putting out less effort to write better reports?

There are two more things I want to mention. In recent months, I've heard of two jury awards, one in the East for $60,000 and one in the West for $250,000, in lawsuits filed by criminal defendants against individual officers and their employers for alleged federal civil rights violations. Both cases had to do with search and seizure problems and issues of probable cause to search a car and make an arrest.

No one wants to have to sell his home and his car to pay damages to some suspected crook. So remember that the same kinds of problems ambiguous reports cause **me** in a criminal prosecution can haunt **you** if you find yourself defending a civil lawsuit. Now go back and review the chapter on Living With Your Report. From time to time, skim through it again.

The other item is this. I recently saw a cop with eight years' service lose his job (and most likely his police career) because of charges he deliberately falsified arrest reports. I don't know whether he did or didn't. But I read several of those reports—"standard" police writing every one—and I could see the department's dilemma, and his.

Read one way, he almost certainly falsified information. Read another way, he was simply guilty of sloppy writing. The dilemma arose because on every disputed statement, there were two possible interpretations of his writing.

That's how critical an ambiguous sentence here and there in a report can turn out to be. It may mean you help a criminal go free, it may mean you lose a lawsuit, and it might even mean you lose your career. If I were you, I wouldn't want to risk any of those possibilities just because I wanted to show everybody that I could write the way police officers have always written.

Everything I've suggested in this book is designed to make things easier on a couple of people (you and me), while making it tougher on a couple of others (the criminal and his lawyer). If I've come on a little strong from time to time, or repeated something until your intelligence was thoroughly insulted, it's because I believe in what I've said, and I think it's important to try to make you believe in it, too.

Criminals keep finding ways to commit their violence and larceny; courts keep finding ways to suppress evidence; jurors keep finding ways to avoid being as tough as the crooks. Law enforcement officers can't afford to maintain any status quo for eighteen years—we've got to find ways to improve at doing our jobs. I think writing better police reports can help.

☐

A CURSE . . .

. . . on training officers and department heads who think the suggestions in this book would make dandy regulations. There's no such thing as dandy regulations. Most of the cops I know don't even want to read a **book** about report writing, much less a bunch of rigorous regulations. Most people just naturally hate regulations. So if you were thinking all the way through this book about how you could turn it into some departmental-format regulations, think again. I've tried to make this book as readable as it could be; if I've succeeded for you, don't ruin it for others by translating it into required-reading bureaucratic regulations. OK?

Notes

America's Most Popular

Practical Police Books

Becoming a Police Officer $14.95
Criminal Law $37.95
California Criminal Codes 2nd$37.95
California Criminal Procedure 4th $37.95
California Criminal Procedure Workbook $19.95
California's Dangerous Weapons Laws $9.95
Community Relations Concepts 3rd $37.95
Courtroom Survival $16.95
Criminal Evidence 4th $37.95
Criminal Interrogation 3rd $19.95
Criminal Procedure 2nd $37.95
Criminal Procedure (*Case approach*) 5th $44.95
Effective Training $29.95
Exploring Juvenile Justice 2nd $37.95
Encyclopedic Dictionary of Criminology $19.95
Evidence and Property Management $29.95
Florida's Criminal Justice System $14.95
Fingerprint Science 2nd $19.95
Gangs, Graffiti, and Violence $14.95
Getting Promoted $29.95
Informants: Development and Management $19.95
Inside American Prisons and Jails $19.95
Introduction to Corrections $44.95
Introduction to Criminal Justice 2nd $44.95
Introduction to Criminology $44.95
Investigating a Homicide Workbook $14.95
Legal Aspects of Police Supervision $24.95
Legal Aspects of Police Supervision Case Book $24.95
The New Police Report Manual $14.95
Natl. Park Service Law Enforcement $19.95
Paradoxes of Police Work $14.95
PC 832 Concepts $24.95
Police Patrol Operations 2nd $37.95
Practical Criminal Investigation 5th $37.95
Report Writing Essentials $14.95
Research Methods $37.95
Search and Seizure Handbook 6th $19.95
Sentencing: As I see it $14.95
Traffic Investigation and Enforcement 3rd $31.95
Understanding Street Gangs $19.95

Shipping costs: $5.00 for first item and 50¢ for each additional item.
Price subject to change

*All prices are quoted in U.S. Dollars. International orders add
$10.00 for shipping.*

Credit card orders only, call:

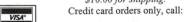

1-800-223-4838

*Nevada Residents add 7.25% Sales Tax
Unconditionally Guaranteed!*
www.copperhouse.com

WITHDRAWN

MEDIA CENTER
ELIZABETHTOWN COMMUNITY COLLEGE
600 COLLEGE STREET ROAD
ELIZABETHTOWN, KY 42701

WITHDRAWN